Using Client Feedback
in Executive Coaching

Using Client Feedback in Executive Coaching

Improving Reflective Practice

Hélène Seiler

Open University Press

Open University Press
McGraw Hill
8th Floor, 338 Euston Road
London
England
NW1 3BH

email: enquiries@openup.co.uk
world wide web: www.openup.co.uk

First edition published 2021

A catalogue record of this book is available from the British Library

ISBN-13: 9780335249411
ISBN-10: 0335249418
eISBN: 9780335249428

Library of Congress Cataloging-in-Publication Data
CIP data applied for

Typeset by Transforma Pvt. Ltd., Chennai, India

Praise for this book

"This book focuses our attention on the controversial and under-researched topic of clients' feedback on the work of the coach. The author has approached this difficult task in a robust manner, addressing both conceptual and practice-oriented issues. Whichever theoretical position the reader might have, I believe that engaging with this book will prove to be developmental."
—Tatiana Bachkirova, Professor of Coaching Psychology and Co-Director of the International Centre for Coaching and Mentoring Studies at Oxford Brookes University, UK

"Having worked as a Senior Executive Coach for more than 25 years I am surprised again and again at how often the coach's and/or the client's feedback is neglected or given rather randomly during the coaching process. Hélène's book is therefore a welcomed insight on how the coach's feedback can be used in a structured manner to help the coach and coachee continuously improve their work together."
—Carola Hieker, Co-Founder and Managing Director of HIL Coaching and Honorary Professor of Transformation Leadership at University College London, UK

"I highly recommend this book to all Executive Coaches, both beginners and experienced practitioners. Hélène has made a strong case as to why 'feedback is the food for champions'. She has presented anecdotal and evidence-based real-life situations that we can learn from. This is a must-have book if one wants to succeed in the highly competitive environment of executive coaching. It provides useful tips, do's and don'ts, and guided templates on how one can constantly grow and become more effective in serving clients via seeking feedback from them."
—Wai K, ICF Master Certified Coach and Managing Partner, JMC Coach Mastery Academy, Malaysia

"A big thank you to Dr Hélène Seiler for having opened a new reflective space for the benefit of coaches and clients. I particularly appreciated the reflective questions offered at the end of each chapter, which function as a tool for self-supervision of one's practice. I was intrigued by the perspectives offered by the representation of the Executive Coaching Behaviour Observation Scale (EXCBOS), featuring trust as a bridge between transformational learning and empathy. Finally, I was touched by the humility

that permeates her works and echoes the necessary humility of the coach, enabling us to truly position ourselves as open and co-responsible. I recommend this book for all coaching practitioners."

—Valérie Ogier, Associate Director,
Centre International du Coach, France

"This book provides a fresh and well-researched perspective on the importance and best practices for seeking client feedback during the coaching process. Both new and experienced coaches will find useful take-aways that can be quickly put to work, improving both the coach's approach and the client's experience."

—Teresa J Pool, ACTP Director, UT Dallas Executive
Coaching Certificate Program, USA

"Hélène Seiler's thoroughly researched book makes a novel and invaluable contribution to the executive coaching literature. In a growing industry, which still has much progress to make towards becoming a profession, Hélène provides a rigorous evidence-based approach that can significantly enhance the development of coaches and contribute to improving the standard of executive coaching."

—Alan Sieler, Director, Newfield Institute and
Ontological Coaching Institute, Australia

Contents

List of figures and tables

Figures

Tables

About this book

Experienced executive coaches serve the needs of high functioning clients in their work context. They know to 'get out of the way in order to be fully available for their client' (Hullinger and DiGirolamo, 2020). They respond to Humberto Maturana's appeal in The Student's Prayer (Zohar and Marshall, 2001): 'You will not know who I am by listening to yourself'.

Coach training organizations emphasize the power of listening to clients, to their presenting issues, and to the worldview that has constructed them. Along their developmental journey coaches become adept at suspending their own judgement. They learn to be increasingly aware of any self-talk that might distract them from achieving unconditional positive regard, a core condition of a successful helping intervention (Wilkins, 2000).

As a result, great executive coaches excel at partnering with their clients to co-design the substance of the coaching conversation. But what about the co-design of the coaching process? How often do they lean on their clients to become better at what they do? According to the few studies that have been published, they rarely do. Instead, they report listening to themselves, their peers, teachers, accreditors, assessors, and supervisors.

Some of you might wonder if this is even a problem. Is there a role for the client in the professional development of coaches? Are clients knowledgeable enough about the coaching process to give actionable feedback to an experienced executive coach?

Some of you might see the benefit in seeking client feedback but are not sure how to make this work. Isn't there a contradiction in taking precious time out of the coaching session to take care of the coach's professional development instead of that of the client? Why not stick to a feedback survey after the session has taken place?

What is this book about?

I have written this book to make the case that we are indeed missing out when we don't ask our clients for feedback during a coaching session, and I offer a process to do so seamlessly. In fact, the book's premise was to turn a proposition on its head: our clients can support our development in the same manner that we can support their development, by giving evidenced-based developmental feedback. But our coach community lives in a paradox. Most of us routinely offer developmental feedback to our clients using, for example, multi-rater feedback instruments that are evidenced-based, meaning that they relay the observation of leadership and managerial behaviours that are demonstratively effective. Yet our clients, who spend the most time observing us in practice, way more than all other observers combined, are not equipped to reciprocate.

My claim is that a client feedback instrument can support the professional development of the coach, if it is based on coaching behaviours that are evidenced-based. Along the way the book substantiates a few additional claims:

- Yes, our clients are able to give us feedback. In fact, they have something important, different, novel to say to us, about the manner with which we conduct the coaching process.
- Yes, our clients are willing to give us feedback. If they don't it's because we lack a common vocabulary to use.
- Yes, we short-change ourselves when we don't ask our clients for feedback.
- Yes, it is possible to solicit client feedback during a coaching session without breaking the flow of the conversation.
- Yes, there is a link between acting on client feedback and an improvement in the quality of coaching. In other words, when we solicit client feedback, we also serve our clients' needs.

Who will benefit from reading this book and why?

I have written this book primarily for executive coaching practitioners, with the intention of helping them become more effective when they work one-on-one with their clients. Supervisors (by that I mean professionals who support the reflective practice of executive coaches) and educators will also find the book useful should they wish to increase the 'share of voice' of the client in service of the professional development of the executive coaches and students whom they serve.

This book is not suitable to assess executive coaches. The client feedback instrument has not been constructed to support a comparison between executive coaches, or between an executive coach and a performance standard.

While life, group or team coaches may find interesting parallels with their practices, some of the coaching behaviours described in this book are specific to one-on-one interactions with executives.

How is the book structured?

The book contains three sections, in addition to this introduction and some parting words. Each chapter starts with a summary of key points, so that you can decide whether it is useful to you to read it in full. It ends with a series of reflective questions so that you can relate its content to your own experience and professional development needs.

Section 1: the case for client feedback

The first section comprises three chapters and makes the case for client feedback. In Chapter 1, I cover the definition of feedback, inviting you, through a few exercises, to reflect on your own experience as a provider and receiver of feedback. In Chapter 2, recognizing that executive coaches hold different beliefs about why and how executive coaching works, I spend some time discussing how one's chosen theory of coaching influences one's views about the relevance of client feedback. In Chapter 3, I make the case for the client as a source of developmental feedback for the executive coach, regardless of one's theoretical orientation.

Section 2: The client feedback instrument

The second section also comprises three chapters. Chapter 4 introduces the content of the client feedback instrument. Chapter 5 focuses on its first component: empathy, while Chapter 6 introduces its second component: transformational learning. In Chapters 5 and 6, a complete list of behaviours warranting client feedback is presented. These behaviours are interpreted in relation to the competency models in use by accreditation bodies and institutions of learning, thus highlighting the complementary nature of the client feedback instrument. The relevance of these executive coaching behaviours is illustrated in relation to two fundamental coaching outcomes: the strength of the coach–client relationship and the generation of new insights for the client.

Section 3: Using client feedback in reflective practice

The third section focuses on how to make use of the client feedback protocol in your practice. Chapter 7 looks at contracting with clients so that they understand why their feedback is important. Chapter 8 discusses when and how to ask for client developmental feedback, and how to use it as a foundation for reflective practice. In Chapter 9, I suggest approaches to use client feedback data in mentoring or supervision settings.

The book concludes with suggestions to get started with client feedback in your practice.

What to expect?

I want to make sure you understand my worldview about executive coaching, because it inevitably impacted why and how I have conceived the client feedback instrument and protocol of administration. As a pragmatist, my belief is that effective coaching is dialogue-bound, co-created by the coach and the client, as the coaching engagement unfolds.

Consequently, I deploy a particular coaching tool or technique if and only if there is mutual agreement that it will service the coaching need of the client. I don't believe that any coaching tool or technique is universally useful, even if it is evidenced-based. I also don't believe that I am the sole coaching expert in the room. After all, most executive coaching clients lead teams and use coaching skills daily. I am open to the possibility that together we might come up with something just right to achieve our common goal. But this does not mean that anything goes. I welcome experimentation as long as the dialogue remains anchored in the sharing of evidence.

I recognize that some of you hold different beliefs. In 2019, I have had the privilege of presenting my research on client feedback in professional conferences and coaching training organizations. I have had fascinating discussions with colleagues who hold different paradigms yet consistently deliver great coaching.

Some of my positivist colleagues believe that it is best to leave the client outside of the professional development of the coach because it distracts from the main purpose of the coaching process. Being in service of the client means applying 'tried and true methods' that have been developed and refined over time by expert practitioners. Consequently, the best way to obtain client feedback is to measure the success of the coaching intervention and eventually go back to the drawing board, between experts, to address potential issues. Indeed, a significant body of research shows that certain techniques consistently deliver when they are executed flawlessly by the coach.

Some of my postmodernist colleagues, who continue to amaze me with their masterful artistry, object to any attempt to model the coaching process. In fact, several qualitative investigations of the client experience indicate that a sizeable minority of clients experience great coaching as something magical, mysterious, even mystic. I personally don't think this is magic but rather the product of cumulative experience in service of the utmost customization of the coaching process.

Whatever your coaching paradigm is, I hope that reading this book will trigger intriguing questions for your reflective practice and deepen your discussions with coaching colleagues, teachers, and supervisors, ultimately benefiting your clients.

SECTION 1
The Case for Client Feedback

1   What is client feedback?

Chapter summary

- Two types of feedback: summative (results) and formative (behaviours leading to results)
- Three definitions of feedback: behaviourist, social, and cognitive-developmental
- Debates about the effectiveness of feedback:
  - To what extent is it impacted by the characteristics of the feedback giver?
  - What about the characteristics of the feedback recipient?
  - Which is more effective: summative or formative, or a combination of the two?
- Most other helping disciplines use a combination of summative and formative client feedback

Purpose of Chapter 1

When you think about feedback, what comes to mind? This chapter reviews the many definitions of client feedback that currently co-exist in the root disciplines of executive coaching, including management, education, psychotherapy, and sports coaching. It uncovers the underlying theories they manifest. It proposes an operational theory of client feedback to support the professional development of the executive coach.

Definition

> *Feedback is the process of communicating a piece of information to someone about what they have done, with the purpose of triggering an intention to change. It comes in two forms, summative and formative.*

Summative feedback

Summative feedback states the result(s) of an intervention. An example, as shown in Figure 1, is a satisfaction survey completed by a client at the end of an executive coaching intervention.

CLIENT EVALUATION FORM – CONFIDENTIAL

COACH	Hélène Seiler
CLIENT	Jane Doe
PROGRAMME	Leadership development with integrated coaching

Please give us feedback about how beneficial you found the coaching provided by Dr Hélène Seiler by rating the effectiveness and circling the appropriate number.

Not at all	A little	Somewhat	Very	Extremely
1	2	3	4	5

Figure 1   Example of summative feedback: a client feedback survey at the end of a coaching intervention

Formative feedback

Formative feedback shares observations of a practitioner in action. These observations focus on certain behaviours, or groups of behaviours, that are expected to lead to a successful intervention. An example of formative feedback for an executive coach would be a live coaching examination during which you are rated based on the observation of a predefined list of behavioural competencies (also called markers) by trained assessors. Figure 2 is an extract from the International Coach Federation (ICF) list of markers. It showcases the behaviours contained in one of the competencies expected at the Professional Certified Coach Level: 'Creating trust and intimacy' with the client

---

COMPETENCY 3: CREATING TRUST AND INTIMACY

- Coach acknowledges and respects the client's work in the coaching process
- Coach expresses support for the client
- Coach encourages and allows the client to fully express him/herself

---

Figure 2   Example of formative feedback: markers for a PCC level accreditation

Theoretical traditions of feedback

In my early years as an executive coach, my preferred methods for delivering feedback to my clients were 360 assessments and psychometrics. I was not alone: in a survey of UK-based executive coaches, 88% said they used such assessments with at least 70% of their clients (McDowall and Smewing, 2009). While this research has not been updated, it is likely that many executive coaches now rely on a much broader range of feedback techniques, just as I do. Maxwell (2016) offers a useful typology of feedback techniques. The process can be considered in relation to where it comes from (internal or external), the time-frame it refers to (deferred, immediate or future), what its purpose is (developmental or evaluative), and what is observed (dimensions or tasks). Let's consider these distinctions in relation to the

Table 1 Typologies of feedback given to the executive coach

Source	**Internal** Self-reflection of the coach		**External** Reflection about feedback received from an external stakeholder such as an assessor, a client, a teacher, a peer, an observer, etc.
Time-frame	**Deferred** Post coaching	**Immediate** During coaching	**Future/feedforward** Example: imagining what an ideal coaching session would look like
Purpose	**Developmental** Example: preparing for the obtention of a credential		**Evaluative** Example: assessment during a live examination for the obtention of a credential
Focus	**Formative** On a set of behaviours that have been identified as effective		**Summative** On an entire coaching session, or a section of a coaching session, focusing on the end result

Table 2 Traditions and typologies of feedback

Tradition	Source	Time-frame	Purpose	Focus
Behaviourist	External	Immediate	Evaluative: better impact	Summative
Social	External	Deferred and feedforward	Evaluative and developmental: better behaviours for better impact	Summative and formative
Cognitive-developmental	External and internal	Deferred, immediate, and feedforward	Developmental: better thinking for better impact	Formative

feedback that an executive coach might receive over the course of their career, as described in Table 1.

The typologies originate in three major feedback traditions: behaviourist, social, and cognitive-developmental, as presented in Table 2.

Behaviourist approach to feedback

The behaviourist definition of feedback was first theorized as a self-regulation process for machines, drawing from findings in engineering research. In cybernetics, a behaviour is collected and compared to a norm, triggering an adjustment if there is a gap (Wiener, 1961). By applying it to human self-regulation and change, behaviourist psychologists define feedback as a two-step data-collection process comprising a behavioural observation and the collection of information about its impact. When the behavioural observation is linked to a non-desirable consequence, it triggers a change in behaviour (Skinner, 1990).

Example of a behaviourist approach to feedback

Jane struggles with time management during her coaching sessions. Although she is committed to ending her sessions with a question allowing her clients to reflect on their learning, she rarely manages to fit one in. On the advice of a peer, Jane decides to artificially end her sessions 5 minutes before the scheduled time by setting a vibrating timer on her smart watch, so that she always has time to include a reflective piece.

Social approach to feedback

Social theorists introduced an additional element to the process by considering the abilities of humans (and some animals) to change their behaviours not just in response to a non-desirable impact, but also by making predictions about how others might respond to future behaviours. Once they have predicted that a change of behaviour will positively impact others around them, they intentionally set a goal to change (Bandura, 1977).

Example of a social approach to feedback

Over time, Jane notices that she tends to ignore the vibrating timer on her wrist. Things are simply too rushed. Her supervisor invites her to reflect on the impact that her time management has on her clients and to experiment with a little trick. How about asking the client the following short question at the end of each session: 'What was your emotion coming into the session and your emotion coming out?' She offers to discuss the results when Jane has enough responses to identify patterns. After surveying a few clients, Jane notices that emotions such as rushed, overwhelmed, excited often come up. She realizes that her time management may at times have a negative impact on her clients. With the help of her supervisor, she sets goals to better manage her time, including doing a process-check mid-session. This will help re-calibrate the agenda for the session as needed, and help her fit in the final 5 minutes of client reflection.

Cognitive-developmental approach to feedback

Constructionists and cognitive-developmental psychologists added yet one more element to the process, which, arguably, is unique to humans: one's own mental model, affects, and comprehension of events (Kegan, 1982). At this level of complexity, feedback integrates behavioural observations, information about one's impact in relation to the social processes at play, and one's own reflection so that the receiver arrives at a decision to experiment with new behaviours. Arguably, these new behaviours are subjected to further feedback and reflection, eventually leading to a higher level of cognition, which will then be challenged again in a series of feedback loops (Kolb, 1984; Nicolaides and McCallum, 2013).

Example of a cognitive-developmental approach to feedback

Jane is making progress. However, when she next talks to her supervisor, she notices that she spends a lot of energy trying to keep time in check during her coaching sessions. Her supervisor invites her to elaborate. Sometimes, she says, 'I wonder if my efforts at time management are a distraction and prevent me from deeply listening to my clients'. Overall, she feels more and more stressed before her sessions and less fulfilled during her sessions. All these time management efforts feel inauthentic to her, as her strength is really to tune in to her clients and go with the flow. Her supervisor wonders to what extent she carries too much responsibility in the management of the session. Jane reflects that she rarely speaks up when she has the intuition that the client is veering off track. The supervisor inquires whether there would be a way to speak up and share how she feels with her clients, inviting them to collaborate on time management. Jane agrees to experiment with a client she knows well. She is surprised to find out that this client welcomes her initiative. He invites her to be even more assertive and push-back when things go off track. Jane is encouraged and starts experimenting with more clients, and progressively learns to let go of the burden of being the sole time manager of the session, leaning more on her clients. Progressively, the sense of rush recedes and the final 5-minute reflection slot seamlessly fits in.

Effectiveness of feedback

In 1996, Kluger and Denisi published a landmark article on the effectiveness of feedback based on a review of the major quantitative studies at that time. While there was some indication that formative feedback was more likely to be effective than summative feedback, the authors cautioned that feedback was not always related to job performance. In some studies, arguably, it was even detrimental to performance. They concluded by calling for more research. In particular they wondered to what extent the characteristics of the feedback giver and/or the feedback receiver influenced the relationship between feedback and job performance.

Characteristics of the feedback recipient

A meta-analytic review of feedback-seeking behaviours (Anseel et al., 2015) concluded that the characteristics of the feedback recipient were significant moderators of the effectiveness of feedback. An individual's levels of self-esteem and self-efficacy were important predictors of their receptiveness to feedback. Individuals who actively sought feedback were more likely to engage in building relationships, networking, and socialization behaviours. Individuals with a strong goal orientation were more likely to accept negative feedback, while those with strong self-efficacy were less likely to view it favourably. In education research, studies indicate that focusing on external formative feedback might be more effective at the earliest stages of a learning process. In contrast, internal feedback might be more successful at later stages of a learning process (Thurlings et al., 2013). In coaching, these findings are yet to be replicated. However, they raise important questions about the readiness of the coach for feedback, which I will explore later in the book.

Characteristics of the feedback giver

Kluger and Denisi (1996) hypothesized that an individual's response to feedback was likely influenced by the credibility attributed to the feedback giver. Peer feedback provides a useful setting to study the phenomenon since peers typically are less knowledgeable than supervisors or direct reports about the content of a feedback recipient's job (Bailey and Fletcher, 2002). One such study demonstrated that when a peer was perceived by the feedback recipient to be more knowledgeable about their job than the average of all peers, their feedback was considered to be more accurate and more satisfactory, and was then predictive of job performance (Jawahar, 2010). These findings have been replicated in coaching research in relation to coach-to-client feedback. Coaches must be seen as credible by their clients for a feedback intervention to be linked to coaching effectiveness (Bozer et al., 2014). We will explore later in the book how the perceived low credibility of clients in the eyes of their coach is an obstacle to the effectiveness of client feedback, and how it can be overcome.

Formative versus summative feedback

Another debate about the effectiveness of feedback centres around the respective merits of observing dimensions (a summative approach to feedback) or tasks (a formative approach to feedback). This debate is particularly lively in the assessment centre literature (Jackson et al., 2012) in relation to the quality of observations by assessors. Proponents of the dimension-based approach assess behavioural manifestations of standardized competencies across a number of work contexts, then make a judgement about the proficiency of the manager. This approach is typically used for the purpose of the annual evaluation of managers and is based on competency models. Critics of the dimension-based approach argue that such evaluations do not provide reliable information because work behaviours are not always consistent (Mischel and Shoda, 1995). In addition, dimension-based assessments are prescriptive and result in a top-down approach that is not well adapted to current organizational contexts, which require a more distributed form of leadership and multiple sources of feedback (Laloux, 2014). Finally, competency models rest on the consensus of opinion of experts, which takes time to obtain. As a result, they might no longer be relevant by the time the evaluation takes place, because requirements may have evolved in the fast-paced world in which organizations operate (Schippmann et al., 2000).

Proponents of the task-based approach assess the quality of unfolding processes and outcomes of a particular task, without passing judgement on behaviours. The major criticism of task-based evaluations is that they cannot be standardized or objective because each situation is unique (Lievens and Christiansen, 2012). Morozov (2016), reflecting on the evaluation system of Uber drivers, which rests entirely on the client's satisfaction ratings after a ride, argued that without a set of objective data to orient the evaluation contract, all that remains is the subjectivity of the most powerful stakeholder, who declares 'the truth' about the value of a particular employee or contractor. This brings back an even more insidious form of command and control than in scientific management, because it is based on power rather than on evidence (Renato Railo, 2015).

Proponents of a mixed-methods approach believe that they have resolved the contradiction based on findings of the Cognitive Affective Personal System Theory (Mischel and Shoda, 1995), which states that individuals activate a stable behavioural scenario based on how they categorize situations. Therefore, it is possible to deliver reliable and valid formative feedback if it is properly contextualized. In some companies, dimension-based evaluations using competency models have completely disappeared in favour of mixed-methods approaches. Yearly evaluations have been replaced by project-by-project, even daily multisource feedback sessions, to allow employees to collect formative data about their performance. As more data is collected, it is hoped that standards will emerge to help link such behavioural data with performance measures (Ewenstein et al., 2016; Cappelli and Tavis, 2018). In the mixed-methods approach, both formative and summative data are used, but they are linked to a specific event, rather than being discussed in absolute terms.

Client feedback in other helping disciplines

In the absence of research in coaching, let us look at how other helping disciplines have approached the process. Intriguingly, most of the root disciplines of executive coaching have a long tradition soliciting and using client or student feedback for the purpose of developing practitioners. With the exception of psychotherapy, the preference is for mixed-methods approaches to feedback.

In higher education in North America, student feedback traditionally consisted of satisfaction surveys at the end of a course – it has since been reconceptualized to measure students' perceptions of teachers' behaviours related to student learning outcomes (Richardson, 2005). While the use of these instruments has been empirically related to an improvement in student learning outcomes in longitudinal research, behavioural change by teachers has not been so conclusive (Onwuegbuzie et al., 2007; Stalmeijer et al., 2008). Research in Europe indicates that this might be related to the format of the feedback process, which is not sufficiently frequent and situational. In Germany, a study of over 300 high school teachers who used a validated student-led, web-based feedback system throughout their course, rather than at the end of the course only, reported a change in teaching behaviours under certain conditions, including more motivated and constructive discussion in supervision (Gaertner, 2014). Similarly, in Australia, action research helped validate an instrument used to study the professional development benefits for teachers of a structured approach to student formative feedback throughout the school year in secondary school settings (Mandouit, 2018).

In educational mentoring, a behaviour scale was developed based on the socio-motivational model and causally linked to the quality of the mentoring relationship and the perceived usefulness of the intervention by the protégé (Brodeur et al., 2015). Brodeur et al. observed that, as a result of receiving formative feedback from their protégés, mentors adjusted their behaviours over time. In particular, behavioural decisions made by mentors became less guided by experts' rules and increasingly tailored to the protégé's needs as the mentoring process unfolded, indicating that the mentor became more responsive to the protégé's feedback interventions.

In sports coaching, practitioners rely on a longitudinally validated 360-degree assessment of coaches that includes students' input (Chelladurai and Saleh, 1980). Empirical research about students' behavioural preferences and coaches' behavioural decisions over the course of a sports season reveals that choices are situational, thus providing a strong rationale for repeated feedback (Höigaard et al., 2008; Fletcher and Roberts, 2013).

In psychotherapy, while client feedback was initially focused on reporting deferred outcomes, the process was re-theorized once it had been established that psychotherapists who request immediate client feedback are more likely to see results than those who do not (Duncan et al., 2010). Consequently, Miller et al. (2015) led the design of an immediate client feedback instrument based on two summative standardized scales measuring client progress on the one hand, and the strength of the psychotherapeutic alliance on the other. Preliminary findings indicate that it is linked to successful psychotherapeutic outcomes if the results are processed through a structured self-reflection process or peer supervision. However, the links between such summative client feedback tools and psychotherapists' behavioural change are not yet conclusive. It is surprising, in light of the findings in other disciplines, that psychotherapy research has stopped short of developing formative client feedback tools. Indeed, a rich body of knowledge linking psychotherapist behaviours and outcomes from the perspective of clients already exists (Norcross, 2010; Levitt et al., 2016). A possible explanation may reside in the fact that psychotherapy research is anchored in a long tradition of scientific and authoritative practice (Levinson, 1996), in which the client may not be considered sufficiently resourceful to offer effective formative feedback.

A preliminary conclusion

Based on what is practised in other disciplines, what would a mixed-methods approach to client feedback look like in executive coaching? It would be based on a predefined set of observable behaviours that are commonly agreed to be effective by the client and the coach. At the same time, the relevance of these behaviours would depend on the desired outcome for each coaching session.

In the next chapter, we will discover that the importance that you attach to the client as a source of feedback, as opposed to other providers such as external assessors, peers, observers or supervisors, depends on your beliefs about what executive coaching is and how it works.

Reflective questions about Chapter 1

Do you ask your clients for feedback? How do you ask? What type of feedback do you seek? How did you come to use client feedback the way you currently do?

What are benefits and drawbacks of client feedback at different stages of the coach's professional development?

Is client feedback for all clients? For all coaches? What are the preconditions of effective client feedback in executive coaching?

2 Coaching theories and client feedback

Chapter summary

- Four theoretical traditions to envision the relevance of client feedback: expertise (mastering key competencies), evidence (using models that have been scientifically linked to positive outcomes), coach-developmental (growing vertically as a practitioner), and client-centred (partnering with the client)
- My own theoretical journey: from expertise-based to client-centred integrative

Purpose of Chapter 2

I ended the previous chapter by suggesting that a mixed-methods approach to feedback, that includes both summative and formative information, would best support the professional development of the coach. From now on, I will refer to the mixed-methods approach to feedback as developmental feedback. This chapter invites you to reflect about the relevance of the client as a source of developmental feedback in your practice by positioning the concept in relation to your espoused theory of coaching. The chapter starts with a review of coaching theories and continues with a reflection on my own theoretical journey as a practitioner. It ends with an invitation to embrace an integrative client-centred theory of coaching in support of the provision of developmental client feedback.

Coaching theory

A theory is the larger framework you have chosen to work with in your practice. It explains why and how coaching works. Not all executive coaches are clear about what it is, and for good reason: multiple coaching theories co-exist and the boundaries with other helping disciplines are not clearly delimited. Cox (2015) identified

Table 3 Theoretical coaching traditions in relation to feedback for the executive coach

Tradition	Source of feedback	Time-frame of feedback	Purpose of feedback	Focus of feedback
Expertise	Experts	Deferred or immediate	Developmental or evaluative	Formative
Evidence-based	Clients	Deferred	Developmental or evaluative	Summative
Cognitive-developmental	Internal, dialogue with experts	Deferred, immediate, future	Developmental	Summative and formative
Client-centred	Dialogue between the client and the coach	Deferred, immediate, future	Developmental	Summative and formative

at least 13 theories, while Bartlett et al. (2014) catalogued no less than 60 definitions of coaching. Thanks to an increasing interest in coaching theoretical research, that number has most likely continued to grow. According to Maltbia et al. (2014), executive coaching will not unite behind a single theory because it is an aggregation and an extension of multiple disciplines with a rich and expanding theoretical tradition including adult learning, adult development, neurosciences, management education, sports psychology, organizational behaviour, behavioural sciences, psychotherapy, counselling, and psychology.

There is no right or wrong way to think about the importance of the client as a source of developmental feedback in your practice; as long as you can justify that your stance is linked to the theory that you have adopted for your practice, that's all that matters. In this section I introduce four important theoretical traditions and examine how they each interpret the professional development of the coach and the role of the client. If your preferred theory of coaching is not included in this review, I invite you to examine developmental client feedback through your own lens. Table 3 summarizes these four theoretical traditions:

- The *expertise tradition* – expects the coach to master key competencies, which is best assessed formatively by experts.
- The *evidence-based tradition* – expects the coach to apply coaching models that have been proved to be effective for the client, which is best assessed in a summative way by using standardized scales completed by the client.
- The *cognitive-developmental tradition* – encourages coaches to engage in a process of continuous self-improvement, so that they can best support their clients. This is best assessed through internal feedback, drawing on both summative and formative information.

- The *client-centred tradition* – views the coach as a partner in the client's learning process, and advises the coach to receive immediate dialogic feedback from their client, placing particular emphasis on the strength of the working relationship.

The expertise tradition

Expertise theorists hold a positivist worldview aimed at the pursuit of truth by scientific means. Experts are the guardians of truth and their knowledge is paramount in the success of executive coaching: in other words, great coaching equals expert coaching, grounded in years of education and practice. This tradition is anchored in scientific management, from which executive coaching first emerged between the 1950s and 1970s (Kilburg, 2016); it then became established in the mid-1990s as it gained status as an intervention to improve the working behaviours of middle and senior management (Feldman and Lankau, 2005). The champions of the expertise tradition describe coaching as a process to achieve agreed-upon objectives within a specific professional context. Often, the focus of the coaching will be to align the capabilities of the executive with the needs of the organization (Stokes, 2015).

Expertise theory was foundational in the development of coach competency models used by coach accreditation bodies. Interestingly, most of these models (including the ICF model) emerged from different disciplines and do not differentiate executive coaching from other forms of coaching. While the root discipline of these models is likely to be psychotherapy or sports coaching, they have evolved based on the same method, a consensus of experts, using job analysis techniques popular in scientific management. As a result, accreditation models are based on an extensive compilation of descriptors of expertise found in multiple disciplines, including – but not limited to – psychotherapy, sports coaching, leadership and management, organizational theory and dynamics, economics, politics, group dynamics and human relationships, individual dynamics, managing diversity and learning, markets and ecologies, behaviour change, expertise development, business problem-solving and human influence, ethics and intercultural awareness (Kilburg, 2016).

The relevance of the expertise tradition, however, is increasingly questioned by those of other persuasions. One issue is credibility and reliability: indeed, multiple and competing competency models co-exist, though they are not always aligned (Blumberg, 2014). Another issue is validity: evidence-based theorists (see below) argue that job analysis is insufficient to guarantee the quality of competency models. They must be measured in relation to their impact on the coaching outcomes. However, efforts to do so have been fragmented, limited in scope, and largely inconclusive (Lai and McDowall, 2014; Maltbia et al., 2014). More fundamentally, research in other helping disciplines has revealed that expert knowledge has little impact on a practitioner's performance (Ericsson et al., 2006). In fact, some wonder if there is even a specialized body of coaching competencies, noting that essential coaching skills such as empathy, collaboration, and positive regard can also be found in the general population of managers (Grant, 2016). Other studies have questioned the specificity of coaching expertise versus psychotherapy expertise. For example, when Bono et al. (2009) compared the practices of psychologist and non-psychologist coaches, they found that there were as many differences in the use of coaching tools between coach-psychologists of different psychologist traditions as there were differences between psychologists coaches and non-psychologist coaches. Consequently, they questioned whether coaches would offer anything that a psychotherapist would not.

The expertise tradition does not view the client as a provider of feedback. It places a lot of responsibility on the shoulders of the executive coach, who is expected to deliver expert coaching seamlessly. Such an approach may lead to a great deal of passivity on the part of clients, a phenomenon that has been highlighted in empirical research focused on capturing the client's experience during a coaching session (De Haan et al., 2013; Myers, 2014). When interviewed about the coaching process, clients typically are hesitant on providing feedback about their coach unless they are explicitly pushed to do so by the researcher. They then show a clear preference for reporting outcomes rather than the coach's actions that led to such outcomes. In other words, clients act as if they do not bear any responsibility during the delivery of a coaching intervention.

The evidence-based tradition

While evidence-based theorists hold the same positivist worldview, they completely disagree about the type of scientific method that is best suited to pursue the truth. They claim that great coaching is indicated by evidence of a benefit for the client rather than the execution of expert coaching skills (Grant and Cavanagh, 2007). Rather than pre-defining dimensions of the coach's expertise, the practitioner is invited to deploy coaching models that are standardized in relation to these measures, leading to a database of successful approaches for the practitioner (Grant, 2016).

Evidence-based theorists hold measurements of coaching effectiveness to very high standards. The 'gold standard' and preferred method is to conduct longitudinal between-subject studies, a research protocol that is commonly used in medical research. In such studies, one group receives a strictly defined coaching protocol (for example, strength-based coaching) which is hypothesized to improve certain leadership characteristics (for example, self-confidence). The other group, the control group, does not receive any coaching. Multiple standardized measures of these leadership characteristics are taken and compared between the two groups, preferably over a long period of time (ideally one year). If the difference between the two groups is considered statistically significant, then the coaching protocol is deemed to be effective in improving the characteristic.

The evidenced-based tradition has been instrumental in the development of a significant body of knowledge about measures of multiple types of coaching outcomes. I relied on their findings to measure the effectiveness of the behaviours contained in the feedback instrument developed in this book. As a result, to ensure that everyone is familiar with the key findings, I summarize them below.

How to measure the effectiveness of coaching

Evidence-based theorists have adapted a model used in the evaluation of workplace training interventions (Kirkpatrick, 1977; MacKie, 2007; Ely et al., 2010). Kirkpatrick's model includes four categories of measures or levels:

- overall satisfaction with the coaching process
- cognitive change
- behavioural change
- organizational change.

Measuring reaction

The reaction or overall level of satisfaction of clients is often used by sponsors to measure the effectiveness of an executive coaching intervention (Mulvie, 2015). For example:

- Rate the effectiveness of the coaching provided by circling the appropriate number (from 1, 'not at all' to 6, 'extremely')
- What did you appreciate about your coaching experience?
- What could have been improved?

This sounds simple enough. Unfortunately, most of us know from experience that the coaching process sometimes holds uncomfortable moments for the client, especially when they have to let go of beliefs and values that no longer serve them (King and Nesbit, 2015). Therefore, satisfaction may sometimes not be a valid measure of coaching success.

Measuring cognitive change

The concept of cognitive change stems from Deci and Ryan's Self-determination Theory (1985). This theory predicts that one's motivation to learn is linked to changes in preconditions that are unique to each individual and are related to their cultural and psychological characteristics.

Meta-analyses of coaching research have convincingly made the case that executive coaching is causally related to cognitive change (Theeboom et al., 2014; Sonesh et al., 2015a; Grant, 2016; Greif, 2016; Jones et al., 2016). Popular measures of cognitive change include the Self-Reflection and Insight Scale (Grant et al., 2002), self-efficacy (Baron and Morin, 2009), self-compassion (Bachkirova et al., 2015), and goal-directed self-regulation (Bozer et al., 2013). Such scales, however, are problematic because they require both pre- and post-coaching measures. And successful coaching interventions may lead clients to experience transformational learning or gamma change, which shifts their conceptualization of the cognitive scale between the time of the first and second measurement (Peterson, 1993).

To avoid this problem in my research, I used a retrospective measure of change, the Serendipity Quotient (McCay-Peet and Toms, 2011), which assesses the generation of new insights, manifested by the occurrence of 'aha' moments. Such moments result from serendipitous connections in the client's brain during a substantive dialogue with the coach, who injects new ideas into the client's thinking system (Kets De Vries, 2013).

Measuring behavioural change

The third level, behavioural change, is often measured in terms of the achievement of individual goals (Clutterbuck and Spence, 2016). But the case has yet to be made that executive coaching has a direct impact on goal achievement. One meta-analysis reported a small effect size of coaching on task performance (Sonesh et al., 2015a). However, two other meta-analyses proffered more cautious conclusions (Greif, 2016; Grover and Furnham, 2016) because of the methodological limitations of some of the studies included. On the one hand, most studies tend to be proximal in nature, which indicates that reported effect sizes may or may not have been sustained in the longer term. On the other hand, they opt for self-evaluation of goal attainment, which is difficult to interpret. Indeed, the accuracy of self-evaluation is moderated by many factors, including personality traits and the conditions under which it is conducted (Mabe and West, 1982). For example, self-ratings are usually more lenient than external ratings (Yu and Murphy, 1993). Additionally, executive coaching has been shown to positively impact self-efficacy (Baron and Morin, 2009), which may in turn inflate self-scores on goal attainment (Nieminen et al., 2013). To counter these biases, best practice is to measure not just proximal but also distal behavioural outcomes and to invite co-workers to rate level of achievement of goals to counterbalance self-assessments (Ely et al., 2010). However, this becomes a very complex endeavour, requiring the collaboration of multiple stakeholders over a long period of time.

Measuring organizational change

The fourth level, organizational change, describes how the executive's behavioural change has impacted the rest of the organization. An example is to measure the level of engagement of the teams they lead. Such measures are rarely taken because it is very difficult to isolate the role of the coach from other contextual elements (Levenson, 2009; Theeboom et al., 2014; Grant, 2014).

Another significant contribution of the evidence-based theorists has been to highlight the importance of the client in achieving the coaching outcome. Psychotherapy research has convincingly demonstrated that the client is a major agent in the success of an intervention. Asay and Lambert (1999) identified four factors that contribute to the variance of the overall outcome of psychotherapy: the client and extra-psychotherapeutic factors (40% of the variance), the relationship between the psychotherapist and the client (30%), the placebo effect or hopes of the client (15%), and finally the theory and technique of the psychotherapist (15%).

Several qualitative and quantitative studies have provided empirical evidence that the model is also relevant to coaching (De Haan and Duckworth, 2013; Smith and Brummel, 2013; Rekalde et al., 2015; Sonesh et al., 2015b). They have shown that clients contribute to the success of a coaching intervention in two ways: through their engagement in the coach–client relationship and through their own characteristics.

The impact of the coach–client relationship on the success of a coaching intervention has been a key focus of evidence-based theorists. Quantitative research has convincingly demonstrated that a strong coach–client relationship increases the likelihood of cognitive change for a coached client (MacKie, 2007; Ely et al., 2010; Lawrence and Whyte, 2014; De Haan and Gannon, 2016). Studies typically use the Working Alliance Inventory to measure the strength of the coach–client relationship, a scale originally developed and validated in psychotherapy research and adapted to coaching (Corbière et al., 2006). The scale measures three elements: the level of bonding, the level of agreement on the tasks involved in coaching, and the level of agreement on the goals of coaching. These three elements were identified by Bordin (1979) as foundational to initiating change in clients of psychotherapy.

In addition, evidence-based studies have highlighted that not all clients contribute in the same way to the success of coaching. For example, in their systematic review of coaching effectiveness studies, Blackman et al. (2016) concluded that the client's motivation for change and self-efficacy impact the success of a coaching intervention. And in a meta-analysis, Grover and Furnham (2016) found that clients' pre-existing knowledge about coaching, the realism of their expectations, and their level of reflection are likely to improve coaching outcomes. Furthermore, two studies by Bozer and colleagues (2013, 2015) indicated that the client's learning goal orientation and feedback receptivity are both moderators of the relationship between a coaching intervention and the client's improvement in self-reported job performance.

Despite the success of the evidence-based tradition in other helping disciplines and its breakthrough in coaching research, it has yet to be embraced by practitioners and sponsors of coaching. To date, as I mentioned in the previous section of the chapter, there have been no concerted efforts to determine the validity of accreditation bodies' competency models by empirically measuring their relationship with coaching outcomes. Large organizations that sponsor executive coaching interventions on a large scale have not shown much interest either. Less than 9% use return on investment (ROI) to assess the results of coaching and the percentage has decreased over the years (Sherpa Coaching, 2018). When interviewed, sponsors of coaching declare that they are not prepared to invest in the assessment of their coaching programmes, citing costs of implementation versus the perceived benefits (Mulvie, 2015). Instead, while organizations that sponsor executive coaching initiatives generally provide evaluative client feedback to the coaches that they contract at the end of the coaching process (Braddick, 2010), they generally limit themselves to summative surveys of clients' satisfaction. Sometimes they track whether goals have been set, and even less frequently, measure progress on goal attainment.

Such hesitation manifests methodological issues that surface when advocating for the systematic use of standardized measures of coaching effectiveness. Indeed, coaching outcomes are sometimes intangible, their production and consumption can occur simultaneously during the session, and they are heterogeneous depending of the needs of the client (Greif, 2016). Maltbia et al. (2014) do not believe that the outcome of coaching is always goal achievement. Sometimes, the coaching process itself is an outcome when it promotes learning, growth, and change. Western (2012) arrives at a similar conclusion when identifying four stances in executive coaching, each requiring the executive coach to learn and practise a specific body of knowledge and skills that lead to differentiated outcomes. The first stance is focused on the inner-self and the personal experience of the client, and aims to develop greater awareness, acceptance, and resourcefulness. The second stance borrows from psychotherapy to reach optimal performance along a continuum of adult development. The third stance identifies which working behaviours need to be optimized in order to maximize personal and team productivity. Finally, the fourth stance holds a mirror to high-level executives and invites them to reflect on ways to optimize their networked self to increase their societal impact.

Increasingly, theorists prefer to view the coaching conversation as a complex adaptive system (Passmore and Fillery-Travis, 2011). In other words, the coaching process is in a constant state of flux and the factors contributing to the effectiveness of coaching influence one another on an on-going basis (Cavanagh and Lane, 2012). This makes a modelized coaching process and the use of standardized coaching models impractical (Bachkirova and Borrington, 2019).

Another major criticism of the evidence-based theory is that it is Western-centric in its choice of outcomes (Coultas et al., 2011). An example is the Intentional Change Theory (Boyatzis, 2006), which claims that a driving force of change for the client is autonomy, so the concept should thus be considered as an outcome of coaching. This might be true in individualist cultures but may not apply to leadership frameworks stemming from other philosophical traditions, such as Ubuntu or Confucianism, which have a more collectivist view of leadership.

The coach-developmental tradition

Coach-developmental theoreticians hold a postmodernist worldview. In their mind, truth is in the eye of the observer and as such cannot be defined universally. Each agent, including the coach, strives to maximize their potential. The coaching space is viewed as a complex adaptive system that cannot be standardized because each situation evolves in its own unique way (Cavanagh and Lane, 2012). Bachkirova (2011) rejects the standardization of outcomes and defines coaching as an emergent process. In particular, reducing outcome to goal attainment in executive coaching is especially problematic for her. Because this is often done in line with the corporate strategy, it may render the coach biased in favour of the sponsor paying for the coaching.

The main benefit of the coach-developmental tradition is to focus practitioners on their reflective self, a space where they can process different sources of information and examine different perspectives in service of their professional development (Hawkins and Smith, 2013). Echoing expertise theory, the most important vessel for improving the quality of coaching is the coach him or herself, potentially supported by another expert. Coaches are responsible for maximizing their ability to create a safe space for the client. However, developmental efforts go much further than the mere development of skills, as advocated by the proponents of the expertise tradition. In the cognitive-developmental tradition, skills are viewed as the tip of the iceberg, a manifestation of a set of foundational capabilities and core values. To strengthen these fundamental characteristics, the coach applies an increasing degree of complexity of thought and reflective judgement about the delivery of the coaching engagement. According to the theorists, this may accelerate the ego-development of the coach, thus increasing their openness, authenticity, and inclusiveness. In sum, rather than accumulating tools and techniques to increase their effectiveness, the coach embarks on a journey of self-development.

The coach-developmental theory has generated a rich body of qualitative research and informed the development of coaching supervision, in that coaches can contract a professional to support their reflective process and professional development. Building on the theories of vertical and adult development in leadership (Kegan, 1982), coaching mastery is defined as the development of capabilities that allow the coach to make informed decisions about which intervention to use and when (Bachkirova and Lawton Smith, 2015). Such capacity is fed by an increasing repertoire of knowledge, skills, and behaviours (Lawrence, 2016), and an ability to deploy creative and improvisational skills (Clutterbuck, 2010). Indeed, at the most advanced stage of a coach's development, there might not exist a direct causal relationship between the coach's choice of intervention and the outcome of the coaching (Bachkirova, 2016).

The major issue with the coach-developmental theory is that, by refusing to use standardized evidence, it renders the developmental process fully subjective. Unfortunately, when there is no common ground to anchor a conversation, power inevitably dictates who will have the last word (Renato Railo, 2015). This is extremely problematic when it comes to assessing, selecting, and accrediting coaches. If there is no standardized evidence to support the evaluation of a coach, then power relations are likely to dictate who will graduate and who will not (Bachkirova, 2016). What happens, and this has been observed in research, is that evaluators are tempted to revert to measuring compliance based on their own preferred model, rather than assessing coaching interventions in relation to what the client needs (Linder-Pelz and Lawley, 2016). Ultimately, the perspective of one expert is inferior to the consensus of a number of experts as promoted by expertise theorists.

Another major issue is an ethical one. What happens when a coach has yet to reach the level of adult development of their client? Laske (2006) suggested that coaches have an ethical duty to abstain. Bachkirova (2011) addresses the problem by stating that adult development, while it is important for a coach, is not always an outcome for the client. Her solution is that the coach becomes aware of their stage of development and engages their skills and abilities in service of the client's agenda accordingly. Such self-awareness is very difficult to achieve in the absence of agreed-upon standards. That being said, it paves the way for attaching greater importance to the client, which is the focus of the fourth and final tradition examined here.

The client-centred tradition

The client-centred tradition holds a pragmatic worldview. It defines the coaching conversation as a reflexive dialogue between the client and the coach in order to achieve a commonly defined task: the personal and professional development of the client (Cox, 2013). The coaching session thus promotes joined meaning-making and joined decision-making (Bachkirova and Lawton Smith, 2015). The client-centred approach emerged from the findings of Rogers (1957), who stressed the importance of empathy for the helping professions, which he defined as understanding how clients perceive the world around them and having the ability to communicate it back to them in a considerate way. In client-centred coaching, empathy is a foundation to support the learning process of the client. The process is anchored in two adult learning theories: Knowles's andragogy (Knowles et al., 2011) and Mezirow's transformational learning (1990). Coaching is thus defined as a learning discipline, in service of four client needs: relevance of the learning, self-direction and control over what is learned, use of own experience as a resource from where to learn, and intrinsic motivation. A skilled coach helps the client ensure that they are secure in their own identity before they can explore new dimensions. Once this is ensured, learning is constructed through a transformational evaluation of experiences. The role of the coach is to support this process by actively and appropriately challenging the assumptions made by the client as they interpret their experiences so that they can move to a new frame of reference. The coach is viewed as a co-creator and a form of teacher in the context of a learning experience. To ensure that the coach is connected to the client's learning needs, the coaching space is fully collaborative. The corollary is that the coach–client relationship, within which the client's learning needs are identified and addressed jointly, is at the centre of the coaching process (Cox, 2015). In the client-centred tradition, Bennett and Bush (2014) have defined executive coaching as an action-learning process to support executives as they sharpen their knowledge and capabilities in service of their most important personal and professional goals.

A major criticism of the client-centred model is that it risks being value-neutral: in other words, if the role of the coach is to support the client's agenda, whatever it might be, what happens when that agenda is immoral or unethical according to the standards of the coach or other parties? (Bachkirova and Borrington, 2019). In addition, what if the client's agenda is overly individualistic? Indeed, it has been argued that the role of the coach might also be to open up the client to their societal responsibilities and not just to their own needs (Hawkins and Smith, 2013).

Another criticism of the client-centred model is that it has not embraced valid measures of the effectiveness of coaching. Measuring the satisfaction of the client is too simplistic: learning is in essence an arduous process, with peaks and valleys. It can be, at times, uncomfortable for the client. Others have wondered whether the satisfaction of the client is really the result of coaching, or simply the by-product of good mutual conversational skills that exist in many other pragmatic endeavours (Bachkirova and Borrington, 2019).

Finally, and most importantly, the success of a client-centred approach is dependent on the readiness of the client for coaching. Some elements of readiness might be specific to the client's stage of adult development, and some might concern the client's system (for example, the client undergoes mandatory executive coaching as part of a leadership development initiative at an inconvenient time). What, then, is the role of coach when these foundations are not in place?

My journey to an integrative client-centred theory of coaching

Each of us has been influenced by a set of historical, cultural, and personal factors as we developed our model of practice. In this section, I will use a narrative approach to describe how I came to choose an integrative client-centred theory of coaching for my practice. This will hopefully achieve two aims: explain what has informed the development of my approach to developmental client feedback, and inspire you to revisit your own theoretical journey as you continue to explore the concept.

I have been an executive coaching practitioner for over 20 years. When I started to coach, I studiously applied various coaching models that I learned in the coach trainings that I had attended. While I sometimes wondered where these models came from, I was not too preoccupied with finding out. Arguably, I was mostly concerned with my ability to develop a satisfied client base. It took me many years of study to gain some clarity about the theoretical foundations of my coaching education. Nowadays, thankfully, most coaching training organizations do a much better good job of articulating the theories that underpin their curriculum. This is partly because over the last 20 years coaching theory has come of age and has developed a body of literature distinct from that of its root disciplines.

During the first 5 years of my practice, I had implicitly adopted a positivist stance to inform my executive coaching practice. I believed that I was largely responsible for the success of the coaching intervention and that my role was to apply tools and models that had a proven track record of achieving the desired outcome for the client. In retrospect, I realize that my implicit stance was a result of my upbringing. Indeed, born and raised in France, I had been 'formatted' to think as an expert, within a positivist, Cartesian paradigm which dominated there in the 1970s and 1980s. After graduating with a Master of Management Science, I became a management consultant in a North American firm, where I dutifully applied myself to deliver advice based on the principles of scientific management.

Cracks had already appeared in my positivist stance when I moved from France to the United States, and it was initially a painful process. Some of the many customs and behaviours I took for granted in France were now observed with curiosity (and sometimes rejection) by my new neighbours and co-workers. I realized that there were different ways of thinking about what is 'true' and became very interested in intercultural awareness. However, when I became a coach a few years into my stay in my new country, I continued to see myself as an expert, happy to have added intercultural knowledge to my bank of expertise.

Looking back, I am thankful for the positivist stance. It was a very useful anchor in my early years of coaching. Expertise and evidence-based coaching models strengthened my confidence and quelled my self-doubts during the coaching sessions, allowing me to focus entirely on what my clients had to say and to support them to the best of my abilities.

It took me another geographical move to shift away from positivism as a coaching practitioner. After spending 13 years in the United States, I lived in Malaysia for almost 7 years. While in South East Asia, I attended two transformational, long-term coach trainings, where I was able to experiment with postmodernist approaches to coaching. Most notably I was introduced to hermeneutics and discourse analysis as methods to explore the subjectivity of the client (Sieler, 2003). In addition, I learned to use the Seven Eye Model of supervision (Hawkins and Smith, 2013), which supports the coach's reflection with a self or guided exploration of a system of multiple perspectives during a coaching engagement. The experience led me to reconceptualize my role as a coach, understand what I could influence, accept what I could not control, and – most importantly – learn how to lean more on my clients to achieve the coaching outcome. Once I had fully internalized that my client was a learning partner, it allowed me to let go of the assumption that I was solely responsible for the success of the coaching process. Instead, I shifted to sharing responsibility with the client. Ultimately, it allowed me to adopt a pragmatic and pluralistic theory of coaching (Clutterbuck, 2010).

Once I understood that I was equally responsible for the coaching outcome with my clients, I started to experience the limitations of the client summative feedback that I received. In fact, these client satisfaction surveys continue, to this day, to generate a great deal of emotion for me, on which I can arguably lean on to discover more about my 'self' as a coach. However, they fall short in providing evidence about what it is exactly that I did to provoke satisfaction (or dissatisfaction) for each of my clients. A few years ago, when I brought up the topic during a supervision session, I was encouraged to experiment with client formative feedback. I welcomed this suggestion because it was a good fit with my coaching stance, which views the client and coach as learning partners.

I adapted my first client feedback template from a supervision model, the Seven Conversations Model of Supervision, developed by Bachkirova et al. (2011). My interpretation of the model consisted in two concurrent, reflective templates. I used the first, the coach's template, to reflect about my behaviours, motives, and results immediately after a session: it proved quite helpful to organize my notes and I continue to use it, most notably in preparation for working with my own supervisor. I gave the second template to my clients and invited them to use it before and after the session to reflect on their learnings in relation to my interventions and to envision how this would inform the next steps of the coaching process.

Over time, I noticed that most of my clients could not always spare the time to use it. However, they welcomed the opportunity to mutually reflect in real time during the coaching session itself. As a result, I started to ask for immediate formative client feedback using the Situation Behaviour Impact (SBI) model (Riddle et al., 2015). The process begins with the contextualization of feedback by linking it with a specific situation; it then reports an observed behaviour and finally discusses its impact. I have noticed that most of my clients are willing and able to give me SBI feedback, and that I get valuable knowledge about the links between some of my behaviours and their impact. That being said, the initial selection of behaviours is based on the subjectivity of my clients, who decide what they want to report back to me.

Perhaps, as a result of this, I noticed that my reaction to feedback was overly driven by the characteristics of the feedback giver. Two examples, which I have reflected on in supervision, can illuminate this phenomenon. When I work with newly promoted strategy consulting partners for the purpose of onboarding them in their new role, this is a territory I know very well. When they give me feedback, it is very difficult for me to let go of an implicit mentoring stance. Therefore, I tend to interpret their feedback as a developmental opportunity for them, rather than for me. At the opposite end of the spectrum, when I started working with Malaysian senior executives in the oil and gas sector, I was largely in unknown territory. Inevitably, I tended to relate their feedback to a developmental opportunity for me, rather than reflecting about what the nature of their feedback said about their own professional development needs.

Pragmatist philosophers such as Dewey and Peirce have warned that when there is no evidence to anchor a dialogue, both parties should seek commonly agreed sets of standards to pre-emptively address conflicts that may arise between them (Diggins, 1994). When no such standards exist, power relations then take precedence (Renato Railo, 2015). Often, it is the coach's aura of expertise that prevails (Stokes, 2015), leaving the client powerless. In the context of client feedback, this is not what I wanted to happen, and I felt the need to revisit and re-embrace positivist methods to inform the development of a client feedback instrument.

An integrative theory to support the definition of client developmental feedback

These reflections planted the seed for developing a theoretical framework that I will describe as client-centred integrative. The integrative client-centred theory defines executive coaching as a dialogue between a professional coach and a client with managerial authority in an organization. A complex adaptive system, it supports the growth of the client through a personalized action-learning process grounded in shared evidence.

As a result, the client feedback protocol that I have developed rests on the client-centred theory of coaching (Cox, 2013), which places the coach and client on equal footing in service of the client's needs. It is anchored in a common vocabulary of effective coaching behaviours and outcomes surfaced by expertise-based and evidence-based methods, thus supporting a mixed-methods approach to feedback. The data collected feeds the reflective process of the executive coach as promoted by cognitive-developmental theorists to improve practice (Bachkirova and Lawton Smith, 2015).

Developmental client feedback encourages transparency and furthers the working relationship with the client. It fosters a productive learning dialogue, where coaches discuss the choices they make with their clients, linking coaching behaviours with coaching outcomes (Drake, 2011; Lane, 2016). While the model recognizes that the coaching process is a complex adaptive system that cannot be modelized, it invites both the client and the coach into a process of continued co-experimentation (Bachkirova and Borrington, 2019), in service of the client's needs.

Reflective questions about Chapter 2

Thinking back about the curriculum of the coach training programme(s) that you attended, what would you say was its main theoretical influence?

Thinking back about your journey as an executive coach practitioner, what is your experience of the strengths and shortcomings of each of the four theoretical traditions: expertise, evidence, coach-developmental, and client-centred?

What is your espoused theory of coaching? How does it position the client in relation to the coach's professional development process?

What is your preferred way to assess your professional development and who do you think is best positioned to measure it?

What is your experience receiving feedback as a coach? Which theoretical tradition(s) influenced the evaluation process that was used?

From your perspective, what is the contribution of the client to the success of coaching?

To what extent do you consider yourself an expert of the coaching process? How does it influence your thoughts about client feedback?

3 The case for developmental client feedback

Chapter summary

- Few executive coaches use client feedback to support their professional development
- Client feedback strengthens the client–coach relationship, a foundation of coaching success
- Client feedback allows the coach to capture data that is different from other sources
- There are two major barriers to soliciting client feedback: the reluctance of the client and the resistance of the coach

Purpose of Chapter 3

In the first two chapters, I defined the concept of developmental client feedback for the executive coach and proposed a client-centred integrative theoretical lens to operationalize it. In this chapter, I make the case that client feedback is beneficial not only to the coach but also to the client and to the coaching outcome. I also review potential obstacles to client feedback, which can be overcome with a common vocabulary of effective coaching behaviours.

Who gives developmental feedback to the coach?

Executive coaches overwhelmingly rely on experts for developmental feedback, which they receive primarily when they undergo training or accreditation. In the Global Coaching Survey conducted by the ICF in 2016, almost all practitioners reported having received some form of coach-specific training, with the majority indicating that they currently hold a credential from a professional coaching organization (ICF/PwC, 2016). In the most mature markets, executive coaches hire supervisors to receive developmental feedback, on an on-going basis, from a qualified professional. For example, over 92% of UK coaches and 83% of Australian coaches report using formal or informal supervision (Tkach and DiGirolamo, 2017).

A qualitative study focused on the perspective of a worldwide sample of coaches on their strategies for lifelong development (Hullinger and DiGirolamo, 2020) highlights the importance of receiving on-going feedback from more experienced coaches, such as peers, mentors or supervisors to feed their reflective practice. The client is noticeably absent as a source of feedback data.

Most coach accreditation bodies include the competency of seeking client feedback in their models but stop short of conceptualizing the phenomenon. In a survey administered to the membership of the European Mentoring and Coaching Council (EMCC), 40% of coaches indicated that they obtained feedback from their clients (Passmore et al., 2018). The question they were asked did not make any distinction between summative and formative feedback. However, further down in the survey, executive coaches were asked an open-ended question about the means by which they obtained developmental feedback and did not cite the client as a source. This indicates that the survey participants most likely equated client feedback with summative feedback.

The general practitioner's literature envisions client feedback as a summative data source to calculate the return on investment (ROI) of a particular coaching intervention. For example, O'Neill (2007) suggested measuring the success of a coaching engagement in relation to the three most important goals that the client wanted to achieve. Thereafter client and coach agree on appropriate measurements, such as, for example, comparing the results of 360-assessments before and after the intervention.

Qualitative research on client feedback, while limited, has produced three protocols: one that is used between two sessions, one at the end a session, and one at the beginning. In the previous chapter, I mentioned my own experience using the first of these three protocols, a guided reflection template for both the client and the executive coach in-between sessions (Bachkirova et al., 2011). The second protocol uses a client questionnaire that reverse-engineers the strength of the coach–client relationship based on a series of questions asked by the coach to the client at the end of a coaching session (Boston, 2013). The questions are intriguing because they were elaborated on the basis of qualitative interviews with clients and coaches. The third protocol, which unfortunately was constructed without any client input, consists of a typology of the different roles a coach could play, and is shared with the client at the start of a coaching session (Bright, 2015).

Most companies that sponsor executive coaching use formative assessments for their employees, but generally back away from formatively assessing their pool of executive coaches in house (Braddick, 2010). Rather, they rely on the advice of referees, such as agencies, who screen executive coaches on their behalf (ICF, 2019). In addition, the vast majority of sponsors limit summative assessments to satisfaction surveys, because they consider that ROI analyses are too costly and complex (ICF, 2019). Some organizations check whether coached executives have set goals, monitoring progress through verbal feedback. There is very little agreement as to what measurements should look like, how to carry them out, and how they could inform the management of the coaching talent pool (Mulvie, 2015).

Developmental client feedback is beneficial to the client

While Chapter 1 reviewed the benefits of developmental client feedback in relation to the professional development of the executive coach, in this section I explore its benefits for the client. Overall, client feedback promotes a stronger client–coach relationship and provides data that is vastly different from that gleaned from other sources.

Client feedback strengthens the coach–client relationship

Regardless of their theoretical lens, researchers and practitioners of executive coaching agree that a strong coach–client relationship is the foundation of successful coaching (De Haan and Gannon, 2016). Importantly, it is the perception of the support received, not reports of the support that was provided, that predicts the effectiveness of the intervention. This phenomenon has been empirically studied in mentoring (Eby et al., 2013), psychotherapy (Bachelor, 2013), and coaching (De Haan and Duckworth, 2013; Kauffeld and Gessnitzer, 2015).

Client feedback strengthens the coach–client relationship because it promotes mutual transparency. Experienced executive coaches typically invite their clients to view the coaching space as safe and encourage them to be transparent. But there is another side to transparency which is the propensity of the coach him or herself to be transparent, by being authentic and forthcoming. A key manifestation of such transparency is the willingness of coaches to be explicit about a tool or technique that they are planning to use. The relationship between transparency and the strength of the working relationship has been empirically studied in most of the root disciplines of coaching. Greater transparency has been positively linked to the strength of the therapist–client relationship in psychotherapy (Miller et al., 2015), the teacher–student relationship in education (Mandouit, 2018), and the coach–athlete relationship in sports coaching (Fletcher and Roberts, 2013).

In executive coaching, we lack similar studies but there are strong indications that transparency has the same effect on the strength of the coach–client relationship. To substantiate this claim, it is useful to return to the concept of the working alliance introduced in the previous chapter. Its three components (bonding, agreement on tasks, and agreement on goals) have been shown to be highly related (Corbière et al., 2006). Coaching studies that have examined the experience of clients giving feedback to their coach and receiving information about the coaching process reported a link between transparency and the strength of the working alliance. In particular, they noted that:

- An increase in client knowledge about the coaching process is likely to increase agreement (Gyllensten and Palmer, 2007)
- The more the coach discuss their choices with the client, the more likely they will be able to tailor their approach to the client's needs, thus achieving stronger agreement (Clutterbuck, 2010; Stokes, 2015)

- Increased transparency about the coaching tools and methods used by the coach encourages the building of rapport and a rebalancing of the coach–client relationship (Boston, 2013)
- In contrast, withholding information about the coaching process increases differences of perception between the client and the coach over time, reducing the level of agreement and ultimately damaging the relationship (De Haan and Nilsson, 2017).

In addition, clients participating in Boston's (2013) study reported that the feedback process gave them an opportunity to improve their delivery of feedback at work. Overall, both the client and the coach accelerated their learning when there was a structured process in place for client feedback.

A case study

Connor (name changed) felt stuck in his role as head of research in a Canadian technology company. He felt trapped in a difficult relationship with his boss, and had few opportunities to showcase his skills. Some of his trusted colleagues had cautioned him that he sometimes came across as resentful and demotivating in meetings. While he had considered looking for another position, he was not sure if he was ready for this considering his current mood. Pat, his coach, suggested that he pen a few stories about past accomplishments. At the next coaching session, they would analyse what he had written to identify themes and patterns in relation to his strengths. To get him started, Pat asked Connor if he would like to narrate and explore one story during the coaching session. Connor agreed, shared his story and reported feeling more optimistic at the end of the session. He also committed to send additional stories in advance of the next session. Pat also felt optimistic. From her experience with multiple previous clients, this appreciative exercise would generate energy for Connor, opening his mind to his strengths and to opportunities to reframe his current role.

However, Connor failed to send anything in. At the start of the next coaching session, Connor shared that the exercise had felt draining to him. He explained that he was future-oriented, craved variety, and the last thing he wanted to do was to relive the past. Instead, he was looking for fresh ideas. He did not want to continue the exercise.

Pat was momentarily perplexed. But suddenly she realized that she had not explicitly shared with Connor what she was planning to achieve with the exercise. Had she done this Connor would have opened up sooner about this learning style. Pat spent a few minutes explaining why she had chosen the exercise and what she was trying to achieve. During their discussion Connor mentioned that he enjoyed the storytelling concept. He wondered if it could be adapted to future-oriented stories as opposed to past stories. In fact, he hoped to be invited to lead an upcoming product development project but did not know how to build his case. Could a future-oriented storytelling exercise about this particular project help?

After telling the future-oriented story Connor reported feeling energized. That same day he initiated a meeting with his boss to put himself forward as project leader, and was subsequently selected.

Clients provide a different set of feedback data to the executive coach

In Akira Kurosawa's film *Rashomon*, a murder is described in four contradictory ways by four different witnesses. The movie title was subsequently used to name a concept, the Rashomon effect, which relates to the notorious unreliability of eyewitnesses.

The Rashomon effect has been observed and described in several coaching studies comparing the perspectives of a client, a coach, and one or more external observers at the end of a coaching session. De Haan and Nilsson (2017), using an instrument measuring the deployment of coaching interventions, concluded that the self-perceptions of executive coaches about the prevalence of their non-directive and client-centred coaching behaviours were significantly more optimistic than those of the client. Incidentally, such asymmetry has been reported during studies of managerial coaching behaviours (Ellinger et al., 2003) in which supervisors do not perceive the frequency of their more directive behaviours at the same level as their direct reports do.

This asymmetry is particularly visible concerning the coach–client relationship. In quantitative studies, in line with findings in psychotherapy research (Clemence et al., 2005) and mentoring research (Larose et al., 2005), ratings of the strength of the coaching relationship by coaches and clients do not correlate (De Haan et al., 2013). Findings from two behavioural studies help understand the phenomenon. In the first study, interactional behaviours were least likely to be perceived by coaches, yet the most acutely perceived by the client (Linder-Pelz and Lawley, 2016). The second study concluded that the perceptions of empathy between the coach and client differ (Kauffeld and Gessnitzer, 2015). In particular, while coaches perceive that their nurturing empathic behaviours are fundamental to the client's perception of overall empathy, their clients favour cognitive empathic interventions to form their perception of the overall empathy of the coach.

Even greater discrepancies are found between clients and external evaluators. In two studies, observers of coaching sessions rated its quality lower than clients and coaches did (Myers, 2014, Linder-Pelz and Lawley, 2015). The researchers indicated that the observers' and clients' descriptions were most compatible when describing the level of coach presence, acknowledging, listening, questioning, and depths of probing. In contrast, they disagreed the most when assessing the degree of confrontation, challenge, probe, direction, and goal orientation given by the coach. Researchers questioned whether these observers were overly influenced by their own coaching models, as they made sense of what was going on during the session. Arguably, another study that compared critical moments of coaching from the perspective of clients, coaches, and sponsors of coaching showed that while clients and coaches agreed on most of the critical moments, sponsors selected different moments (De Haan and Nieß, 2015).

Reflecting on a study of multiple coaching pairs observed in action by experts, Myers and Bachkirova (2020) summarized the complementarity of observations:

- Clients tend to report positively about the coaching process as long as they experience positive outcomes.
- Coaches tend to report their in-session decision-making the most positively, referring to best practices that they had successfully enacted.
- Observers always evaluate the quality of the coaching session more negatively than clients and coaches. They do not observe certain events that held a shared meaning for the coach and the client, unless these moments have been explicitly described by them during the session. In the absence of such a contextualization, observers revert to their own frame of reference and critique specific aspects of the intervention which are relevant to them, but may not be relevant for the particular pair that they had just observed.

Two further studies indicate that clients may notice certain coaching behaviours more frequently than others, regardless of the range of behaviours displayed by the coach. Between 2013 and 2015, the Coaching Research Institute (Tonomura et al., 2018) measured the prevalence of a list of predefined coaching behaviours as observed by executives during their coaching process ($N = 215$). Coaching behaviours related to empathy and bonding were more frequently observed than behaviours related to changing the client's perspective. De Haan et al. (2016) surveyed 537 clients about their perceptions of a predefined set of clusters of coaching behaviours. They found that supportive behaviours were more often observed than informing, confronting, and prescribing behaviours.

In summary, clients observe some coaching behaviours more than others, and they tend to relate them to moments of insight for them. In contrast, coaches relate to how successfully they have been implementing best practices, while observers look at their own models, and how these could have been more productive than those chosen by the coach they have just observed.

Barriers to client formative feedback

While soliciting summative client feedback is a given, most executive coaches I spoke to during my research and subsequent conferences and webinars reported that it is not easy to receive formative feedback from a client. This might explain why it is not prevalent, as I reported at the start of the chapter. This section will examine two important barriers to soliciting client formative feedback: the reluctance of the client and the resistance from the coach.

The reluctance of the client

In the previous chapter, I mentioned that evidence-based researchers have convincingly demonstrated that the characteristics of the client play a large part in successful coaching. This manifests the agency of the client. Skilled coaches will often activate it by inviting their clients to take ownership of their issue and become resourceful. However, clients observed in research seem reluctant to extend their agency to the coaching process itself. In some instances, and especially if the working alliance with the coach is not strong, they revert to a passive-negative approach by resisting an intervention that they don't understand or feel uncomfortable with, especially if the coach is not transparent about it. The fact that satisfaction is often the only summative piece of feedback that they are offered to share does not help the process as it may strengthen the halo effect that many clients experience in coaching. As a result, clients may be tempted to avoid any uncomfortable situation which might damage the level of satisfaction that they aspire to maintain (Stokes, 2015).

More broadly, in multiple research settings, clients appear to have difficulty pinpointing exactly what the coach has done to give them a sense that the interaction was going well (De Haan et al., 2010; Myers, 2014). They show a lack of interest, and even sometimes discomfort to describe which coaching techniques and formal processes had taken place. They prefer talking about moments when they experienced satisfaction or dissatisfaction, and when some learning moments occurred for them. Because clients markedly hesitate before identifying specific interventions or behaviours of the coach leading up to or during a critical moment, De Haan and his team wondered whether clients held back because they feel incompetent or because they really do not perceive anything at all. In sum, very few of the clients who describe positive critical incidents refer to anything the coach has done. In addition, the research team noted that clients seem less interested in making sense of what is happening in the building of the relationship than in describing what is happening for them. It seems as if they do not recognize that their coach played a direct role in building the relationship or contributed to the outcome.

Power relations inevitably develop during a coaching process (Welman and Bachkirova, 2010). At the start of a coaching engagement, when the working alliance is still being built, most clients tend to hold back on sharing too much information about themselves. They may unconsciously overpraise the coach as a way to protect themselves and stay psychologically safe (Stokes, 2015). While the client's level of self-disclosure may increase over time, the halo effect concerning the coach appears to linger. Indeed, clients interviewed in research speak highly of their coaches, of their own positive experiences, and of a number of benefits that they have experienced throughout the coaching process. But when probed further, it becomes clear that some sort of confirmation bias is taking place (Myers and Bachkirova, 2020). For example, clients always assume that coaches know what they are doing and that, if something does not feel right, it is probably because they are ignorant of the coaching process. For example, there are instances when clients assume that the coach understands their concerns when the coach later admits to not understanding them. In another instance, the client assumes that their unsettling experience during a coaching session was due to them rather than the coach. For instance, the casual dress of a coach that was considered by everyone present in the room to be slightly shocking was later redefined by the client as thought-provoking. An empty chair exercise was first described as uncomfortable, but recategorized as a necessary evil.

To give themselves permission to break barriers and work at a higher level of disclosure, clients need executive coaches who can create a safe space and build trust rapidly (Cox and Jackson, 2014). Therapy research has demonstrated that the building of trust needs to be modelled explicitly by the coach, particularly at the start of the process, which requires them to show some level of vulnerability. Indeed, it cannot be assumed that the client will drive the process, especially when they are new to coaching (Birnie, 2019).

The resistance of the coach

Unfortunately, many executive coaches, even if they profess a client-centred stance, are under pressure to satisfy both the client and the sponsor of coaching, who sometimes have contradictory views about the desired coaching outcome. In addition, the expertise tradition of coaching remains prevalent in the industry, which leads many executive coaches to bear too much responsibility for the success of coaching, including in the reconciliation of clients' and sponsors' agendas. To protect themselves, they may engage in self-deception which manifests itself in dominant coaching behaviours and a refusal to engage in a dialogue with the client about their choice of intervention (Bachkirova, 2015). This undermines their ability to show an appropriate level of vulnerability and create a safe space, with the risk of reinforcing protective behaviours from the client in return.

When they take too much responsibility for the success of the coaching, executive coaches might also discount the wisdom and knowledge their clients have about the coaching process. As I mentioned in Chapter 1, findings from feedback research (Jawahar, 2010) indicate that the feedback giver must be perceived as knowledgeable about the job of the feedback recipient in order for feedback to be effective. As a result, if an executive coach does not view their clients as knowledgeable, they will tend to discount any unsolicited feedback that they provide. Alternatively, they may ask clients for formative feedback but only on managerial coaching behaviours that they are certain that their client can already master, such as active listening, presence or direct communication (Backus, 2018).

Yet, several studies indicate that the client's knowledge about the coaching process increases as it unfolds (Karboul, 2014; Jones, 2015). For example, Jones (2015) noticed a shift in clients' ability to recognize typical coaching behaviours between the first and the final session. While a novice client will most likely expect and observe consulting behaviours, a more experienced client starts expecting and noticing facilitative behaviours, and in particular those related to promoting the quality of the working alliance.

Unfortunately, clients need to be encouraged to give feedback in the early stages of the coaching intervention. Indeed, findings from psychotherapy research indicate that client feedback is more important at the beginning of treatment than during its later stages. Successful psychotherapists are more likely to ask for and receive early negative feedback about the quality of their work than the average practitioner (Duncan et al., 2010). This allows them to surface and address potential problems at the start of the relationship, before the motivation of the client declines (Miller et al., 2015). In contrast, average practitioners commonly receive neutral feedback at the start of the relationship. However, they risk disengagement later in treatment once it is too late to restore the damaged relationship.

The need for a client feedback protocol

To break barriers and unlock the potential of client formative feedback as early as possible during the coaching intervention, the only way forward is to provide a common vocabulary of effective executive coaching behaviours to both the client and the coach. This will be the purpose of the next section of the book.

Reflective questions about Chapter 3

Do you frequently devote time to explain to your clients the process that you are going to use? What benefits have you observed?

Have you ever observed a Rashomon effect as an observer of a coaching session? What were the key differences between your observations, those of the coach, and those of the client?

How do you feel when you receive negative feedback from a client or an observer? What is your first reaction? How do you manage yourself during the process?

Have you observed that your clients become more knowledgeable about the coaching process as the engagement unfolds? What are the signs that they have increased their understanding of it? How can you better leverage this?

SECTION 2
The Client Feedback Instrument

4 Introduction to the client feedback instrument

Chapter summary

- From the perspective of the client, effective coaching encompasses both empathic and transformational learning behaviours
- Empathic behaviours include cognitive, sharing, and nurturing empathy
- Transformational learning behaviours include preparation, creativity, goal alignment, and maintenance of trust
- The skilful combination of empathic and transformational learning behaviours strengthens the working alliance between the client and the coach and leads to new insights for the client

Purpose of Chapter 4

In the previous three chapters, I defined and operationalized developmental client feedback and made the case that it was likely to support the professional development of the executive coach. I also acknowledged that there are barriers to soliciting client feedback and suggested that a common vocabulary of effective behaviours, a client feedback instrument, might overcome such obstacles. Here, I explain how the client feedback instrument was constructed and introduce its overall structure.

Existing coaching scales

When I decided to construct the client feedback instrument, I started with a critical analysis of the existing body of knowledge. As I mentioned in Chapter 2, multiple coaching competency models and scales exist and have been built from the stance of experts, without the contribution of clients. This can be problematic when building a client feedback instrument, since behaviours may be overlooked that are

Table 4 Existing coach competency models and scales in relation to a client feedback instrument

Critical analysis	Risks
Models and scales are not consistent – they sometimes present contradictory information	Which model is accurate? How to choose a model?
Models do not always distinguish executive coaching behaviours from managerial coaching behaviours or life coaching behaviours	Which behaviours are really specific to the executive coach?
Competencies are sometimes expressed as behaviours, sometimes as outcomes	How to reverse-engineer competencies when they are expressed as outcomes?
Models were developed with coaches and experts only, to the exclusion of the client	Since we know that clients observe differently than coaches and experts, are all the coaching behaviours included in the models useful to clients? Are any behaviours missing?
There has been, to date, no effort to statistically measure whether the behaviours contained in the models are linked to coaching outcomes	Do models include behaviours that might be perceived as effective by coaches as experts, but actually do not lead to positive client outcomes?
	Reciprocally, do models exclude behaviours that might not have been perceived as effective by experts, but actually lead to positive client outcomes?

deemed to be important by clients. There are also other issues with the models and scales, which I summarize in Table 4.

The construction of the client feedback instrument

To address these issues, I decided to engage in further research, using a combination of qualitative and quantitative approaches, called a mixed-methods design (Creswell, 2010).

The first, qualitative strand of the research involved clients in the design of an executive coaching scale. It was conducted between March and May 2017 with five focus groups of experienced clients of executive coaching. The 24 participants were tasked with reviewing and reducing a long list of executive coaching behaviours which I had compiled from a critical review of existing models and scales. To achieve this objective, the focus groups used a method adapted from task analysis, echoing the method used by accreditation bodies when they develop competency models with experts. Working in a sequential manner, the focus groups made changes to the list and ranked its behaviours using two commonly used criteria in task analysis: importance and difficulty (Cadle, 2012). *Importance* was defined in relation to coaching outcomes such as trust in the coach, the generation of new insights, and the attainment of goals, which are commonly used in summative research (Grover and Furnham, 2016). *Difficulty* characterized behaviours requiring specific coaching training in order to achieve mastery. The task analysis process ended once saturation was achieved, at the end of the fifth focus group. The end result was a new scale of behaviours representative of effective executive coaching according to clients.

The second, quantitative strand of the research confirmed the quality of the scale and was conducted between April 2017 and January 2018. I surveyed 107 executives undergoing a 3–4-month coaching programme. At the end of the programme, participants were asked to what extent they had observed the coaching behaviours contained in the scale.

In addition, they were asked to what extent they had experienced three important coaching outcomes: the strength of the working alliance measured with the Work Alliance Inventory (WAI) (Corbière et al., 2006), the generation of new insights for the client measured with the Serendipity Quotient (SQ) (McCay-Peet and Toms, 2011), and a goal attainment measure. As you might recall from Chapter 2, the WAI measures the strength of the working alliance between the client and the coach, based on an estimation of their level of agreement and bonding during the coaching process. The SQ measures the emergence of serendipitous connections in the brain, a precursor of creativity. It has been used to measure cognitive change as a result of a learning process. The goal attainment measure was chosen to measure behavioural change resulting from the coaching process.

The first step was to assess the quality of the scale for the purpose of soliciting client feedback by considering the following two criteria:

- Do these behaviours considered together actually represent a coherent and self-contained coaching process?
- Are these behaviours actually effective?

To answer the first question, I used a statistical method called principal component analysis, a procedure which reduced the set of behaviours contained in the scale even further and surfaced clusters of behaviours (called components) that can be clearly interpreted in relation to the executive coaching process.

To answer the second question, I measured whether the reduced set of behaviours had a statistically significant relationship with the three coaching outcome measures that I had used in the client survey. The set of behaviours showed a positive, significant relationship with both the WAI and the SQ. While the relationship with the goal attainment measure was positive, it was not significant.

Having assessed that the set of behaviours did in fact represent a coherent coaching process and that it was statistically related to two important outcomes of coaching, the WAI and the SQ, I could confirm the quality of the scale for the purpose of soliciting client developmental feedback. I called the scale the Executive Coaching Behaviour Observation Scale (EXCBOS).

An overview of the client feedback instrument

The EXCBOS contains 21 behaviours representing two coaching processes: empathy and transformational learning. I want to reiterate that the EXCBOS is not intended to replace the competency models used by coach accreditation bodies. It has another purpose entirely: that of starting an informed dialogue with your client about what you could do to be more effective. It is not an evaluative instrument, which typically compares coaches and predicts whether or not they will contribute positively to the success of coaching. Such instruments are typically built using different types of samples and statistical methods. Figure 3 presents a graphic representation of the two components of the EXCBOS.

The following two chapters will introduce each of the two components in depth, starting with a definition and exploration of the concept they represent and continuing with a description of their representative behaviours. Obviously, there are many other effective executive coaching behaviours and I don't want to claim that the EXCBOS is exhaustive. Instead, my claim is that the EXCBOS contains representative behaviours that allow executive coaches to take into account the client's perspective in their professional development. These 21 behaviours are an entry point for engaging in more reflective practice.

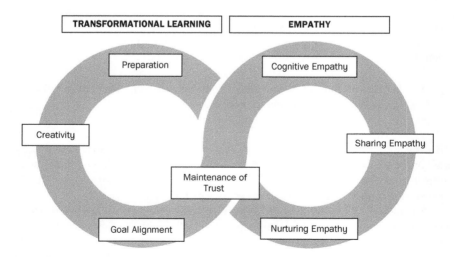

Figure 3   A graphic representation of the EXCBOS

Reflective questions about Chapter 4

What surprised you the most about the construction process of the client feedback instrument?

What is your reaction to the fact that clients identified empathy and transformational learning as the two most important specific executive coaching processes?

Before reading the following two chapters, how do you interpret these processes?

5   Empathy

Chapter summary

- The EXCBOS contains three facets of empathy: cognitive, sharing, and nurturing
- When observed by clients, the empathic behaviours contained in the EXCBOS are likely to increase their experience of a strong working alliance with their coach
- The working alliance provides the foundation for the client's cognitive change

Purpose of Chapter 5

This chapter presents the first component of the EXCBOS, empathy. The concept is revisited from the perspective of the client, building on the research I conducted as well as other studies that have focused on describing the client's experience of the coaching process.

Empathy: The client's perspective

Let's focus on the first component of the EXCBOS that I described at the end of the previous chapter. It has three facets, as shown in Figure 4.

Empathy features prominently in coaching competency models used by accreditation bodies and systematically surfaces in research. The concept is defined by Rogers (1957) as our understanding of how others perceive the world around them and the ability to communicate it back to them in an appreciative manner. Bachelor (1988) distinguished four facets of empathy:

- Cognitive empathy: the understanding of how a person feels and what they might be thinking

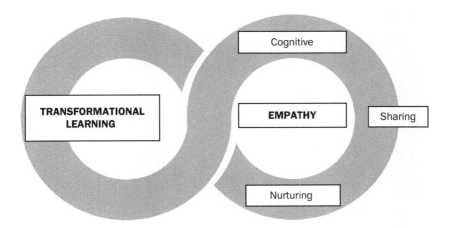

Figure 4 Facets of empathy in the EXCBOS

- Affective empathy: experiencing the same feeling as someone else
- Sharing empathy: communicating back our understanding to the other person
- Nurturing empathy: manifesting a sustained, attentive, and caring presence.

Note that the EXCBOS does not contain manifestations of affective empathy. This might be surprising at first: the word compassion, whose Latin roots literally mean 'suffering with', is often associated with good listening or coaching in coaching competency models. However, let's remind ourselves that these models have been built by experts. Multiple studies of the client's perspective in coaching and other helping disciplines tell a different story. In particular, while cognitive, nurturing, and sharing empathy have been linked to the strengthening of the bond between the client and the coach (Will et al., 2016), affective empathy is generally not perceived as a bonding behaviour by those who are on the receiving end of a helping task (Marjanovic et al., 2012).

In the following sections of the chapter, I will unpack each facet using three lenses:

- A reminder of the general definition of the term
- Selected client quotes, extracted from transcripts of the focus group members who helped construct the scale
- Empathic behaviours contained in the EXCBOS, expressed as a question from the coach to the client

Cognitive empathy

Cognitive empathy describes the ability of the coach to deeply understand what their clients thought and felt individually and in relation to their working context.

In clients' words

It's acknowledging, it's testing, it's asking questions for clarification, it's engaging ... with the person you are speaking to. So, it's asking-for-clarification-questions and saying, you know if I understand what you are saying it's this. Or for me it could mean this.

It's picking up on these emotional cues and going at the pace that the client wants.

Cognitive empathic behaviours in the EXCBOS

To what extent:

- Was I responsive to your needs?
- When you shared something, did I maintain a good balance between over-reaction and stayed overly neutral?
- Did I remain open-minded to what you said?

Sharing empathy

Sharing empathy represents the ability of the coach to play back what they heard in a more concise form.

In clients' words

They make you say something in one minute that would have taken 20 minutes!

There were times when she had clearly explored some of the [comic book] characters I was referring to, and some of their character traits, so as to you use them to explain in your coaching journey what was going on. She was quickly able to bottom line where you were at, what was going on.

What was wonderful was that she would reference things that weren't in my stated goals, but that I had talked about, from like several sessions ago, and like bring them back to things I am currently saying – and that I had forgotten about – and that's a good thing – I do think that – it's not just even note-taking, but it's like a paying attention.

Sharing empathic behaviours in the EXCBOS

To what extent:

- Did I acknowledge your emotions when discussing a topic?
- Did I communicate authentically, transparently, honestly?

Nurturing empathy

Nurturing empathy allows the client to feel safe in the relationship: it creates a protected space. It relates to the concept of unconditional positive regard which was introduced by Wilkins (2000) as a way to strengthen the self-acceptance of the client, without which change is very difficult to initiate.

In clients' words

[She] was absolutely there to help me in the interaction. I can feel she was on my side, if there is a problem.

If the environment is created in the safe space and I understand that she is only there – all she is thinking about in these two hours is how to help me – then there is a positive pull for me to put things on the table.

They really are your partner, your true partner, they are not there, in their own mind they are not assessing you, they are not judging you.

At no point did the body language or the words that were used make me feel like, I was made to feel stupid or being judged differently than how I was judging myself and I thought that was quite powerful.

Nurturing empathic behaviours in the EXCBOS

To what extent:

- Did I show positive regard?
- Was I supportive?
- Did I remain non-judgemental?

How do empathic behaviours impact the outcome of coaching?

During my research, I was able to replicate results found in other studies: cognitive, nurturing, and sharing empathic behaviours strengthen the working relationship between the client and the coach (O'Broin and Palmer, 2010; Myers, 2014; Blackman et al., 2016; Will et al., 2016).

In Chapter 2, I mentioned that the strength of the working alliance between the client and the coach is generally measured by the Working Alliance Inventory (WAI), a scale first developed and validated in psychotherapy research and then adapted to coaching (Corbière et al., 2006). The WAI measures both the level of bonding between the coach and the client, and the level of agreement between them.

Empathic behaviours influence bonding, a concept related to trust. Trust is a heuristic leading to a decision about the level of vulnerability one is willing to display in a relationship *vis-à-vis* the risk of doing so, within an uncertain context (Atkinson and Butcher, 2003).

In clients' words

The art of the relationship: how you build the connection, how you weave this together with humanity and feeling ... maybe I'll use the word genuine.

One that was key is did not make assumptions or judgements about me, I think that's a very important one and it's actually very impactful, because it builds trust.

It takes a lot for some people to trust a complete stranger, and the stranger and the coach have to some way communicate [about] holding the space sacred.

As I alluded to in Chapter 3, coaching research has convincingly demonstrated that coaches' assessments of the prevalence of their empathic behaviours are not linked to the strength of the relationship experienced by the client. Instead, it is only the perception of empathic behaviours by the client that predicts the strength of the working alliance from their perspective (O'Broin and Palmer, 2010; De Haan et al., 2013, 2016). This means that the coach can only hope to influence the strengthening of the working alliance and must seek the perspective of the client (Ianiro et al., 2013; Kauffeld and Gessnitzer, 2015, De Haan and Gannon, 2016).

Measuring the strength of the working alliance from the perspective of the client is therefore critical. While the working alliance is not typically viewed as a coaching outcome, it functions as an amplifier of other coaching behaviours. For example, there is ample empirical evidence that, the stronger the working alliance, the more likely more challenging coaching behaviours will generate new insights for the client (MacKie, 2007; Ely et al., 2010; Lawrence and Whyte, 2014; De Haan and Gannon, 2016; Seiler, 2019). In Figure 5, the handshake symbolizes the working alliance and its central role in the coaching process, from the perspective of the client.

In the next chapter, we'll concentrate on the second component of the EXCBOS, the transformational learning process.

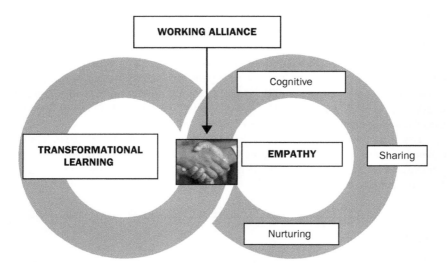

Figure 5   The working alliance and the EXCBOS

Reflective questions about Chapter 5

What surprised you the most about the first component of EXCBOS? Which behaviours and facets did you most expect and which did you least expect?

Which empathic facets and behaviours do you consider as your strengths? What has been your experience of their impact on the coaching outcome?

Which empathic facets and behaviours do you consider as developmental opportunities?

6   Transformational learning

Chapter summary

- The EXCBOS contains four facets of transformational learning: preparation, creativity, goal alignment, and management of ruptures of trust
- The skilful combination of empathic and transformational learning behaviours strengthens the working alliance between the client and the coach
- Transformational learning behaviours lead to new insights for the client, paving the way for cognitive change
- Transformational learning behaviours are not directly linked to behavioural change for the client. It is likely that the client and system are more influential

Purpose of Chapter 6

This chapter presents the second component of the EXCBOS, transformational learning. Similarly, the concept is revisited from the perspective of the client, building on the research I have conducted as well as on other studies that have focused on describing the client's experience of the coaching process.

Transformational learning: The client's perspective

The EXCBOS consists of four facets: preparation, creativity, goal alignment, and maintenance of trust, as shown in Figure 6.

Transformational learning was conceptualized by Merizow (1990). It evokes a fundamental change in one's beliefs, values, and/or feelings leading to a learning event. In the context of a coaching process, clients examine their assumptions

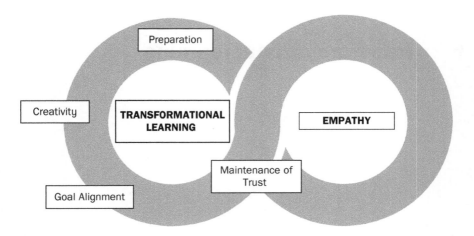

Figure 6   Facets of transformational learning in the EXCBOS

Table 5   Clients' expressions of transformational learning behaviours

Transformational learning behaviours in competency models	Transformational learning behaviours modified by clients in the focus group
'Asked the client how they typically approach change'	'Invited me to reflect about how I typically approach change'
'Was knowledgeable about the client's organization'	'Asked questions about my organization to better understand the issues I presented'
'Allowed periods of quiet reflection'	'Offered periods of quiet reflection'
'Pointed out possible unconscious motives for my actions'	'Encouraged me to think about possible unconscious motives for my actions'

about the situation they presented. As a result, they gain new awareness about themselves and others. Subsequently, they become more resourceful in dealing with the presenting issue, because they have moved to a new way of thinking and being (Kets De Vries, 2013; Sammut, 2014; Moons, 2015; Theeboom et al., 2017).

Coaching competency models used by accreditation bodies and coach training organizations include transformational learning behaviours. However, a closer look at the expression of these behaviours indicates that they tend to be stated in a directive manner. In contrast, clients interviewed in the research expressed them in a more inviting manner, as presented in Table 5.

Such differences in expression evoke a preference for co-designing the coaching process rather than passively accepting the tools or techniques proposed by the coach. Remember that the clients who participated in the research already had experience of coaching. These are the voices of clients who have already witnessed a coach in action. As I remarked in Chapter 3, novice clients are more likely to expect their coach to take the lead. That being said, most clients will grow out of this after the first or second session.

Below, I will unpack each of the four facets of the transformational learning component, by providing:

- A reminder of the general definition of the term
- Selected client quotes, extracted from transcripts of the focus groups that I conducted in research settings
- Representative behaviours contained in the feedback instrument, expressed as a question from the coach to the client.

Preparation

Preparation is a process during which relevant information is discussed by the client and the coach to fully understand the coaching topic and its context. Preparation was identified by Dewey (1910), in the context of the pragmatic endeavour, as the process of knowledge acquisition for the purpose of getting any task done. The preparation process is a key anchor to the adult learning process (Kolb, 1984), and is routinely used by coaches in the early stages of their interventions (Maxwell, 2016). During the preparation process, executive coaches develop new knowledge about the client's context which will increase the quality of their decisions as the coaching conversation unfolds (Senge et al., 2015).

Arguably, clients go beyond the provision of information to the coach during a session. They also deepen and develop their own discoveries by answering reflective questions proposed by their coach (Cox, 2013; Hawkins and Smith, 2013). Such reflections set the stage for the self-determination of the client, allowing them to consider their current circumstances in light of their ideal self (Boyatzis, 2006).

In clients' words

[It's important for the coach] to take risks for the client, for the sake of your client, in your questions.

[There is] a bit of testing and experimentation – and checking back on that testing and experimentation.

[The coach is] forcing you to either be more transparent or thoughtful about yourself, or, pushing you to think about some of the root causes behind observed actions, and compare it to whom you really want to become.

The organization is featured as a contextual element in the preparation phase in alignment with a pragmatic view of workplace learning (Cox, 2013). Some clients actively seek to reflect about their own developmental needs in relation to their employer's business culture and strategy. Others prefer their coach to take the initiative. Either way, this requires the coach to display an adequate level of knowledge about the organization. As Cox summarized, 'application [of learning] depends upon the background knowledge the coach has' (2013: 47).

In clients' words

You might be able to experiment with a more vulnerable approach in the workplace. Is that a good idea, or not? You would want to understand a little bit about the context, or to understand how hard that's going to be, for the client. It depends on understanding the kind of work environment they are going to get back into.

If I see on a spectrum between somebody who truly deeply understands my organization and someone who truly deeply understands me: she understood me and what I needed and demonstrated that much more than she demonstrated an understanding of the organization, so I almost felt like she was a little bit outside the context of the organization.

Preparation behaviours in the EXCBOS

To what extent did I ...

- Check if my understanding of your organization was sufficient?
- Invite you to explore how you approach change?
- Ask questions about your organization to better understand the issues you presented?
- Invite you to state your personal vision for your role in the organization?
- Invite you to explore unintended consequences of your actions?

Creativity

The creativity process describes a reflective dialogue used to generate serendipitous connections between thoughts in the client's thinking system, evocative of an extended cognition (Cox, 2015). This type of dialogue has been described by evidence-based theorists such as Grant (2016), who have considered the coaching process as a space to develop self-determination, a precondition to achieve the self-efficacy required to come up with creative solutions to new problems (Bandura, 1977). In addition, multiple qualitative investigations of the coaching process from a client-centred and coach-developmental lens have identified the creativity process as an integral part of the coaching process, labelling it 'inspiring action' (Hooijberg and Lane, 2009: 488), 'creating resonance' (Moons, 2015: 52), or the 'ability to identify patterns' (Myers, 2014: 187). Kets De Vries (2013) argues that creativity comprises two distinct processes: illumination (where the client is in reflecting mode) and verification (where client and coach are in active discussion). He also compares the co-active engagement of the coach and the client during this process to those of jazz musicians during an improvisation set: 'using their talent for reconstruction, reformulation and respectful listening, [coaches] improvise on the themes their clients present, recasting motives, phrases and statements to recreate experiences in new and interesting ways'. In addition, he views the coach as a 'cloud manager', an integrator of 'multiple ideas, fantasies, representations and relationship patterns' (2013: 153).

As you will see in the following extracts from the focus group transcripts, clients evoke two coaching techniques to trigger creative breakthroughs: inquiry and advocacy.

In clients' words

DESCRIBING INQUIRY-BASED TECHNIQUES

[Imagine] a session where you go and hoping someone is going to say, oh well ... here is the answer, you just need to do it like this: this is your problem and here is the solution. It was very interesting how the space was cleared for me to come up with my own answers if you like, both having the advice request being put back to me in question and sparing personal stories, and the neutrality.

The coach has to sit back, and really let the executive let the solutions emerge from the dialogue ... [it] requires a lot of self-restraint.

It was more about asking the right questions, she was very good at that ... She knew how to ask the right questions, that would help me see which direction I should go to, which decisions.

DESCRIBING ADVOCACY-BASED TECHNIQUES

If the coach does not challenge, then you are just in your comfort zone, you might lead [the coaching session] and have all the answers yourself but not arrive at anything new.

[People like me] they don't know what they are doing because they often never have been told.

[We discussed] how do you prepare yourself and therefore work and develop the skills and the behaviours that will help you move to the next level [and] where he thinks I am using all the skills that I need for the current position.

She could draw analogies with other contexts, which made me feel that not only she was understanding mine but she was also helping me normalize what was for me a particularly unusual working culture.

She was able to help me see the kind of qualities and skills that I have and that I am trying to develop are actually critical to the organization and to move up in the organization, so for me that was a huge leap of development right then.

A good coach will tell you, 'honey, you are not ready', or help you understand: what do you need to get there?

That's my personal opinion, it might be different from anybody – but I expect the coach to give me back some things, to help me get better, to help me improve what I do, not necessarily just be, you know, just be the psychotherapist: basically, let you speak and so on, to get a feel comfortable, because I don't need that, personally. And so, I, it's about getting better, or realizing how to address potential behaviours that could compromise [your career] and in fact are.

The coach that I had used himself as an example: and some of it was business and some of it was personal, and it was always relevant to me.

Many coach training organizations still encourage their students to refrain from giving advice to their clients, even if the International Coach Federation (ICF) has mellowed somewhat on that front. Indeed, the latest version of the competency model published in 2019 recognizes that advice can be good when it broadens the perspective of the client. There is a fine line between informing a client and advising a client. A coach who knows when not to cross the line between the two will be an effective advocate. A review of the coaching literature (Blackman, 2006) notes that advocacy behaviours such as the management of expectations of the client and immediate feedback to the client will be highly effective if delivered by a credible coach.

In clients' words

If you look at a journey as qualifying as a coach, so of course I am hearing ... don't give answers [to the client], don't do and don't, don't, don't, don't. But in terms of my experience [as a client] if we specifically agreed, let's go into that mode, it was very, very helpful, if we hadn't had done that, it would have actually compromised what we were doing, I think a little bit, rather than helping, which is what it did.

The whole value in the process was about understanding behaviours and what was useful was seeing, was for her to spot patterns, and then get me to reflect upon how I'd felt upon seeing that pattern and join the dots and my reflections on how it made me feel, how I felt about this particular period of working life: that was very strong.

She would on occasion reflect back what she was hearing, which might be just a reflection of what I had actually said, or it might be identification of patterns – hum – and sometimes those patterns would come across to me as gentle challenge: is this really the way you want to be?

Creativity behaviours in the EXCBOS

To what extent did you observe the following?

- When you requested advice, I checked first if this is what you really needed and then invited you to reflect on your request.
- I used experiences from coaching engagements in other organizations to broaden your perspective.
- I used examples from my own life story to illustrate a point you made.

Goal alignment

Because of the future orientation of coaching, the setting of measurable goals is considered an important outcome of the coaching process. In fact, most coach competency models feature goal-setting skills prominently (Bartlett et al., 2014) and most coaches report using goal-setting and monitoring behaviours liberally (Vandaveer et al., 2016).

Most of the clients who participated in the research did not say that action planning and goal monitoring were unimportant, but they questioned whether they were specific to the executive coach skill set, arguing that they could complete these tasks by themselves or with the support of co-workers. This point of view reinforces the research of Clutterbuck and Spence (2016), who argued that coaching may be better adapted to the exploration and achievement of 'mid-level goal constructions', which they describe as 'intention or personal striving', rather than the achievement of performance-oriented goals.

In clients' words

There would have been times she would ask me if this is really what is going to make me happy; and if what I, how I am struggling, how I am trying to behave, I am trying to achieve within my organization is really what I wanted myself long term and we discussed these kinds of things quite helpfully.

The ones I like are the 'coachings' that teach me, how to be more me, and manage myself more, better, efficiently, with less hassle, and I think that is good for the organization as well.

Goal alignment behaviours in the EXCBOS

To what extent did I …

- Invite you to reflect on the alignment between your goals and the goals of your organization?
- Invite you to reflect whether your organization's culture enables or hampers your development goals?

Maintenance of trust

The transformational learning process may at times be uncomfortable or draining, especially when the coach challenges the client's assumptions leading to a momentary disequilibrium (Kets De Vries, 2013). Such periods of discomfort may lead to ruptures of trust. We have seen in the previous chapter that clients tend to underreport these occurrences, requiring that the coach becomes more transparent and creative so as to strengthen their trustworthiness (Moons, 2015).

Maintenance of trust behaviours in the EXCBOS

To what extent ...

- Did I invite you to discuss concerns about confidentiality?
- When unable to provide expertise, acknowledged it?
- When shifting from inquiry to advisory mode, I made it explicit?

How do transformational learning behaviours impact the outcome of coaching?

In this section, I will discuss two main benefits of transformational learning behaviours. The first benefit, which may come as a surprise, is that it strengthens the working alliance between the coach and the client as much as empathic behaviours do. The second benefit is their impact on the cognitive change of the client.

The impact of transformational learning behaviours on the working alliance

In the previous chapter, I made a link between empathic behaviours and a strong working alliance between the client and the coach. However, while important, empathic behaviours are not the only ones to strengthen the working alliance.

Arguably, empathic behaviours are foundational to a trusting coaching intervention, but they are not sufficient in executive coaching. Transformational learning behaviours contribute as much to building the working alliance as empathic behaviours do. According to the results of my research, if a coach only displayed empathetic behaviours, devoid of any transformational learning behaviours, they would most likely have only half of their potential impact on the working alliance. Other studies show similar results: all effective coaching behaviours, not just empathic behaviours, play an important role in strengthening the working alliance (De Haan and Gannon, 2016). For example, Baron and Morin (2009) demonstrated that the coach's ability to help the client make connections between ideas was a predictor of changes in the strength of the working alliance. More recently, a within-subject study (Ianiro et al., 2015) showed that combined measures of the working alliance with behavioural observations at different stages of the coaching process supported a causal link between a number of coaching competencies and the strength of the working alliance from the perspective of the client. In particular, a dominant-friendly behaviour from the coach was positively correlated to the perception of the strength of the working alliance of the client when measured after the first and after the last coaching sessions. Finally, a meta-analysis showed that the degree of facilitative behaviour of the coach positively affects the client's efficacy and trust in the coach (Grant, 2016).

These findings echo those of psychotherapy research, which relies on a rich body of empirical study linking psychotherapists' behaviours with client outcomes (Norcross, 2010; Levitt et al., 2016). Such competencies as 'identification and understanding of personal patterns', 'professional structure provided during the session', 'clear discussion of the respective roles', and 'invitation to the client to take the lead' were all related to the strength of the working alliance.

How is this possible? Arguably empathic behaviours create trust, which in turn strengthens the working alliance. However, trust does not just arise out of affect, once the recipient views the actions of the other party as a manifestation of genuine care and concern for their welfare. Trust also arises from cognition, once the recipient assesses that the competency, reliability, and dependability of the other party are deemed sufficient (McAllister, 1995). In fact, McAllister suggests that cognition-based trust might be likely to cause affect-based trust, which in turn predicts bonding. Consequently, trust in the coach is built not only through empathic behaviours but also through the professional credibility of the coach.

In clients' words

You are a coach: I could be a coach too, you know. [For] 30 years I have been doing this teaching and coaching people to go in the right direction. So why is it that you are qualified – that is to me the question always at the back of my mind – that maybe sometimes is a barrier to break.

You absolutely have to be honest [about what you know], if you don't the credibility starts to decrease.

Atkinson and Butcher (2003) added temporality to the model of trust by studying two related concepts, impersonal trust (based on roles and reputations) and personal trust (based on interpersonal relations). They argued that impersonal trust, because it emerges from cognitive and rational assessments, can happen relatively quickly in a helping relationship. In contrast, personal trust is rooted in subjectivity and affect and takes longer to develop. This claim might explain why coaches enrolled in the quantitative part of my research study obtained very high scores on emphatic behaviours. They may have wanted to overplay empathic behaviours so that personal trust developed faster, because the time-frame of the coaching intervention was short (3–4 months).

As you might remember from Chapter 2, the other facet of the working alliance is agreement. The coach plays an important role in developing agreement by deploying a range of influencing tactics. Lewis-Duarte and Bligh (2012) empirically linked the choice of influence techniques by the coach to the level of commitment of the client in the coaching relationship. They distinguished four behavioural dimensions related to influence: inspirational tactics, coalition tactics, consultation, and rational persuasion.

Notice how influencing tactics feature prominently in the EXCBOS. For example:

- *'used examples from other engagement to broaden my perspective'* alludes to consultation
- *'invited me to state my personal vision'* evokes inspiration
- *'invited me to explore unintended consequences of my actions'* corresponds to coalition
- *'invited me to reflect on the alignment between my goals and those of my organization'* amounts to rational persuasion.

Transformational learning behaviours in relation to successful coaching

In Chapter 2, I mentioned that the success of a coaching intervention was measured at four levels: satisfaction, cognitive change, behavioural change, and organizational change. I argued that cognitive change and behavioural change are the two levels that are most useful in highlighting the role of the coach in successful of coaching. In Chapter 5, we established that empathic coaching behaviours impact the working alliance, which itself is an accelerator of coaching success, and may thus indirectly impact all levels of the model.

However, in my research, empathic behaviours were not directly related to cognitive change or to behavioural change. Instead, the EXCBOS was only related to cognitive change, and exclusively through transformational learning behaviours. These findings echo research conducted in other helping disciplines. According to Sternberg and Lubart (1995), preparation, creativity, and goal alignment behaviours encourage clients to change the representations and assumptions they held previously in order to solve a problem. In addition, they might support the emergence of a new relation between concepts related to the problem, thus triggering creativity. Specifically, informing behaviours, because they influence the encoding, recategorization, and recombination of concepts, have been linked empirically to the generation of new insights (McCay-Peet and Toms, 2011). Concerning maintenance of trust behaviours, previous research has shown that ensuring on-going safety in the relationship is related to cognitive change, especially through the strengthening of self-efficacy (Bandura, 1977). Likewise, safe and positive coaching approaches when giving feedback to the client have been linked to creativity (Fredrickson, 2001).

The links between the EXCBOS and behavioural change for the client were inconclusive. While the EXCBOS impacted the likelihood that the client would develop a set of goals, it did not impact the likelihood of success in reaching those goals. Yet, participants almost always reported having achieved their goals. This indicated that other factors were at play, which I will now explore in more depth.

First, many clients, when asked about it, tend to overestimate the achievement of their goals. A first probable cause is the halo effect, and a second probable cause is self-efficacy, which often increases as a result of a coaching intervention, and results in overestimation of performance (Nieminen et al., 2013).

Second, the context of the coaching engagement plays a role. If the coaching engagement takes place in a supportive culture, clients are more likely to receive strong support from their system. The context in which my research took place is a case in point. Participants were enrolled in a workshop at the start and at the end of the coaching process which emphasized appreciative inquiry techniques. Such techniques encourage them to focus on their ideal self, rather than on their 'ought' self (Boyatzis and Howard, 2015), as they prepare for their coaching session. It could have positively impacted their intrinsic motivation to achieve goals regardless of the coaching process itself (Sheldon and Elliot, 1998).

The strong intrinsic motivation of the participants most likely impacted the choice of goals selected. Indeed, the vast majority of reported goals demonstrated more of a learning orientation than a performance orientation. Learning-oriented goals typically create a virtuous cycle as they increase the intrinsic motivation of the participant even further (Dweck and Leggett, 1988; Kasser and Ryan, 1993).

These findings indicate that clients value the coach's interventions because of their impact on the working alliance and on their cognitive development, not so much because of their direct role in the achievement of goals. When it comes to behavioural change, 'it takes a village', as the saying goes. This has profound implications for executive coaches as they balance their choices of intervention. How about less goal monitoring, in favour of a deeper exploration of the unique mechanisms that underlie the client's learning process? Or, how about more goal nudging, inviting the client to be more resourceful in activating themselves and their own support system?

How about, in more general terms, more humility on the part of coaches and more responsibility for clients in the achievement of their goals? After all, it is likely that our tools and techniques may contribute no more than 15% to the success of the coaching intervention, as has been demonstrated in psychotherapy (Asay and Lambert, 1999). Let's make sure we actually achieve our effect by focusing on what really makes a difference for the client: empathy and transformational learning.

Now that we have covered the 'what' of client feedback, let's focus on how to make it happen, which is the purpose of the third and final section of the book. The next chapter will present how to introduce client feedback in the context of the contracting process of the coaching engagement.

Reflective questions about Chapter 6

What surprised you the most about the transformational learning component of the feedback tool? Which behaviours and facets did you most expect and which did you least expect?

Which transformational learning facets and behaviours do you consider as your strengths? What has been your experience of their impact on the coaching outcome?

Which transformational learning facets and behaviours do you consider as developmental opportunities?

What are your views of the respective roles of the client and the coach in achieving the coaching outcome?

SECTION 3
Using Client Feedback in Reflective Practice

7   Contracting for client feedback

Chapter summary

- The formal contract sets the logistical parameters of the coaching engagement. It is a suitable setting to inform the client about the feedback protocol
- External parties, and not just the client, must agree to the process and be briefed about confidentiality
- Contracting includes obtaining informed consent, orientation to empathic behaviours, and orientation to transformational learning behaviours
- Cultural norms of the client must be examined to ensure that the process will benefit, rather than hinder, the coaching process

Purpose of Chapter 7

In Chapter 3, I mentioned that clients interviewed in research appeared uninterested in describing coaching behaviours. In addition, they showed a tendency to hold back in case a coaching intervention made them feel uncomfortable, assuming that the coach is an expert and they are not knowledgeable enough to interfere (Myers, 2014). This chapter gives you a chance to level the field by educating your client about effective coaching behaviours during the contracting process of the coaching engagement. It also discusses cultural considerations with respect to client feedback.

A review of the contracting process

Before discussing how to create awareness about effective coaching behaviours during the contracting process, it is worth revisiting the concept itself. The coaching contract has been defined as 'the collaborative determination of logistics, parameters and frameworks of the coaching foundation' (Gettman et al., 2019: 46). In executive coaching, it includes the clarification of the roles and expectations of multiple parties including the sponsor and/or the direct supervisor of the client (Turner and Hawkins, 2016). It is not a fixed parameter and may require renegotiation as the executive coaching engagement unfolds. For example, the client's job may evolve, requiring a change in the scope of the engagement or the on-boarding of new stakeholders.

Separately, the psychological contract (Rousseau, 1998) refers to assumptions that are made by the coach and the client about the nature of their working alliance as the coaching engagement unfolds. It usually surfaces new issues that were not visible during the contracting phase, need to be made explicit, and will likely lead to revisiting a few elements of the coaching contract. An example of a client assumption is that the coach is responsible for monitoring their progress: if the coach does not follow up with them, they assume they have nothing else to think about or to do. An example of a coach assumption is the belief that the client is committed to solving their presenting issue and ready to explore solutions with them. This type of assumption typically stems from a failure to explore whether unsolved and unexpressed competing commitments are holding the client back. Experienced executive coaches actively investigate the nature of the psychological contract by uncovering and exploring these assumptions throughout the coaching engagement.

This chapter focuses on how to use the coaching contracting process to introduce your client to the client feedback protocol. The next two chapters will demonstrate how client feedback can also highlight issues related to the psychological contract.

Informing about client feedback

Orientation of external parties

The sponsor and other relevant external parties must be informed first that you are planning to solicit client feedback during your coaching engagement(s). To make your case, the content of Chapter 3 will help, as will the text box in the next section of this chapter.

Once external parties have agreed, you must insist that your feedback data remain confidential between you and the client. This is very important because, as I mentioned in the previous chapter, the EXCBOS is not intended to compare executive coaches against a given standard let alone to predict future performance. Instead, it is to be used by the coach to support their own professional development. Doing otherwise will lead to errors (Seiler, 2019) that could damage the coaching culture in the organization. If external parties are interested in screening or assessing their executive coaches, which is perfectly legitimate, they must use a different tool.

Orientation of the client

For your clients, I suggest a three-step approach during the contracting phase. The proposed approach assumes that your client already has some knowledge about

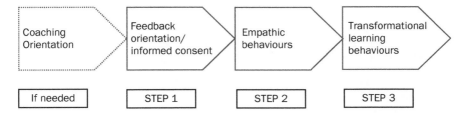

Figure 7 Contracting for client feedback

executive coaching, such as through the orientation sheet they would have received from the sponsor ahead of time. If this is not the case, introduce your client to executive coaching first. Don't make it too complicated or long. Bear in mind that clients undergo a very fast learning curve once exposed to coaching. Even novice clients who first expect coaching to look more like consulting or counselling will recognize empathic and inquiry behaviours as early as the second session (Karboul, 2014; Jones, 2015; Seiler, 2019).

The contracting process is summarized in Figure 7. In step 1, you make the case for client feedback, share the key logistical aspects of the process, and obtain informed consent from your client. In step 2, you introduce empathic behaviours. In step 3, you introduce transformational learning behaviours. I recommend providing your client with written documentation about the process so that they can refer back to the information as needed. Suggested templates are presented in the following sections of the chapter.

Step 1: Feedback orientation

The box below is an example of an orientation sheet used to present the business case, high-level logistics of client feedback, and obtain the informed consent of your client. It can also be adapted for the sponsor and other external stakeholders of the executive coaching process.

Client feedback in my practice

My clients spend the most time observing me in practice, way more than all other observers combined. Research has shown that client feedback is unique and complementary to *The business case*

the type of feedback I can receive from external evaluators and peers. I believe that your feedback will help strengthen my effectiveness as a coach even further, benefiting you and other executives I work and will work with.

I use a protocol to solicit feedback from clients. It is anchored in an instrument which will invite you, during some of our *What to expect* coaching sessions, to report your observations regarding the frequency with which I have displayed effective coaching behaviours, and the impact these may have had on the coaching outcome. When used, the administration of the feedback instrument adds about 5–10 minutes to the coaching session.

The process is completely confidential, and the information you share with me is for my eyes only. Should I wish to share my scores with another professional, I will not share any information about you and will ask you first.

Confidentiality and privacy

If you agree to the principle, I would like to spend the next few minutes introducing the behaviours that are contained in this instrument.

The request

In fact, you might be interested in this review for your own development as a leader, since managing people often invokes coaching skills. As we move along the coaching process, I'll be happy to discuss these behaviours further with you should you find it useful.

The benefits

At the same time, I can assure you that if you prefer not to give me any feedback in this manner, this will in no way adversely impact the quality of our work together.

No pressure to participate

Step 2: Orientation to empathic behaviours

Experienced clients are likely to be aware of the benefits of empathic coaching behaviours (De Haan and Nilsson, 2017; Tonomura et al., 2018; Seiler, 2019). In contrast, novice clients may at first be surprised by these behaviours, as most expect dispassionate advice (Karboul, 2014). However, once they have experienced empathy, they quickly recognize its importance (Jones, 2015). Be prepared to spend more time with certain novice clients during the contracting session. As needed, offer to discuss again at the end of the first or second session.

Table 6 provides an information sheet that you can paraphrase and leave with your clients at the end of the contracting session.

Step 3: Orientation to transformational learning coaching behaviours

To introduce transformational learning behaviours, I recommend describing the coaching process as a series of learning loops that unfold over the course of several sessions (Cox, 2013). First, an issue is presented by the client and the coach and client explore it together (preparation). Then, the coach and client brainstorm to trigger new insights and learnings from the client (creativity). This typically leads the client and the coach to design experiments during which the client will display new behaviours in the working context and observe how it impacts them and others

Table 6 Orientation to empathic coaching behaviours

What empathy will look like	How this might impact you
I will stay open-minded to what you say	You will be heard and you will share your perspective
I will show positive regard	You will have a chance to explore the positive aspects of your situations
I will communicate authentically, transparently, honestly	You will receive an external perspective, independently of what you may want to hear
I will be supportive	You can explore all of your ideas with me, even if they seem far-fetched
I will be responsive to your needs	You can be transparent about what you need
I will remain non-judgemental	You can share anything that you feel is important without fear of being judged
I will acknowledge your emotions when discussing a topic	You will gain greater awareness about your emotions and how they might be perceived by others
I will neither over-react nor stay overly neutral	You have the space to explore any issues without being concerned about my own emotions

(goal alignment). As the conversation unfolds there might be ruptures of trust that need to be addressed (maintenance of trust). Between this session and the next, the client will most likely engage in the experiment(s) that have been co-designed. The learning resulting from such experimentation may become the starting point of the next coaching session, and so on.

Preparation behaviours

Preparation behaviours will be well understood by experienced and inexperienced clients alike. In fact, sponsors often prefer to select executive coaches who have previous experience in the industry or the company so that they can rapidly understand their clients' working reality and cover the preparation phase (Braddick, 2010). While clients expect that their coach will ask clarifying questions to better understand their context and submit to this gracefully, they won't necessarily appreciate the impact these questions might have on their own reflective process. You might want to point this out as an additional benefit for them when you introduce the preparation behaviours.

Creativity behaviours

To introduce this section, start by making a clear distinction between prescribing skills and informing skills (Heron, 2001).

Table 7 Orientation to preparation behaviours

Typical preparation behaviours	Why they are important
I will check with you whether my understanding of your organization is sufficient when discussing an issue AND I will ask questions about your organization to better understand the issues you present	If I have an adequate understanding of your work context, we will be able to assess together, when you present an issue, what you can control, what you can influence, and what you can simply notice and accept
I will invite you to explore unintended consequences of your actions	This will be useful to expand your self-awareness
I will invite you to explore how you approach change	We all learn differently: we need to design a coaching process that fits your style
I will invite you to state your personal vision for your role in your organization	You will be more likely to reach your goals if you can clearly link them to your personal vision

Table 8 Orientation to creativity behaviours

Typical creativity behaviours	Why they are important
When you request advice, I will check first if this is what you really need and then invite you to reflect on your request	My priority is to ensure that you are resourceful
I will use experiences from coaching engagements in other organizations to broaden your perspective AND I will use examples from my own life story to illustrate a point you made	These are ways I might be able to help you generate new ideas

Prescribing means giving advice. Prescribing behaviours are considered counter-productive in relation to a coaching process (Cox, 2013). On a side note, Backus (2018), who interviewed experienced coaches, reported that they generally experience giving advice as a manifestation of their performance anxiety, which leads them to deploy prescribing behaviours to address their own needs for reassurance.

Informing means injecting information into the client's thinking system to create serendipitous connections in their brain, thus triggering creativity. It is done in support of the client's reflective process, usually happens after a period of mutual exploration, and is very effective (Whitworth et al., 2007; Kets de Vries, 2013).

Goal alignment behaviours

Most novice clients expect their coach to take a prominent role in helping them set goals and monitor their progress. This is not what the experienced clients who participated in the focus group said. They mentioned that their executive coach was much more helpful in brainstorming experiments to help them achieve goals they had usually defined themselves. Coaches were more helpful when they debriefed these experiments by focusing on the impact that they had on the client and on others in the organization, rather than when they attempted to monitor progress. Clients may also be ambivalent about the nature of the goals they should set and the coach has an important role to support their thinking process. In their review of the literature about the use of goals in coaching, Clutterbuck and Spence (2016) concluded that a systemic approach to goal-setting seemed more adapted than an individualistic approach to address the fast-changing and complex systems in which executives operate. In fact, individual goals that are misaligned with group goals have been linked to poorer group performance (Minski, 2015).

Orientation to maintenance of trust behaviours

It is useful to warn the clients that uncomfortable moments are sometimes part of the learning process. The three behaviours below will help address some situations during which ruptures of trust between the client and coach might occur.

Table 9 Orientation to goal alignment behaviours

Typical goal alignment behaviours	Why they are important
I will invite you to reflect on the alignment between your goals and the goals of your organization AND I will invite you to reflect whether your organization's culture enables or hampers your development goals	We both want to assess whether your goals are realistic and fit in the company culture. If this is not the case, you may want to explore whether you have the power and influence to change the company culture

Table 10 Orientation to maintenance of trust behaviours

Typical maintenance of trust behaviours	Why they are important
I will invite you to discuss concerns about confidentiality	Worrying about confidentiality might prevent you sharing relevant information with me
When unable to provide expertise, I will acknowledge it	It is important that you obtain the information you need
When shifting from inquiry to advisory mode, I will make it explicit	Leading questions will be banned so that you can reflect free from undue influence

Feedback across cultures

Cultural traits are developed throughout our life in the multiple groups we live in, such as country of birth, family, communities, and the organizations we work for. They include accepted beliefs, conventions, customs, social norms, and behaviours associated with each particular group (Van Nieuwerburgh, 2016).

With regards to client feedback, cultural traits may impact the effectiveness of client feedback in two ways:

- The effectiveness of the coaching behaviours themselves (for instance, direct cultures may not be as responsive to appreciative inquiry, while hierarchical cultures may not respond well to inquiry-based approaches to learning)
- The general attitudes of the client regarding giving and receiving feedback.

Effectiveness of coaching behaviours in different cultures

Research in this field is still emerging and is, in my opinion, unlikely to produce definite results because the issue can be approached through divergent lenses. Positivist researchers have attempted to measure the impact of the client's cultures on the coaching outcome. Postmodernist researchers argue that each client is at the convergence of so many different cultures, that it is impossible to isolate the impact of one particular cultural trait: coaching effectiveness needs to be considered one client at a time.

So far, the results of evidence-based research are inconclusive (Grover and Furnham, 2016). My own research is a case in point. The sample included about 30 different nationalities, but I did not find that the citizenship of the participant impacted how executive coaching behaviours were observed or how these influenced the coaching outcome.

As a pragmatist practitioner, I encourage you to identify, first during the contracting phase and then on an on-going basis throughout the coaching engagement, whether your clients' responses to your coaching behaviours may or may not be nested in cultural values. My own experience working with hundreds of clients worldwide over the last 15 years has taught me to refrain from making any assumptions that an individual from a particular country would behave in a certain way. Let me give an example based on national culture, though the same may apply from multiple other cultural dimensions such as ethnicity, gender, and so on. During the 7 years I lived in Asia, only a minority of my Asian clients did not display collectivism (Hofstede, 1980), a trait that makes you believe that individual fulfilment is secondary to the group's needs. Likewise, my Asian clients did not systematically display power distance, a trait which leads the client to feel less knowledgeable than the coach and more likely to accept their expertise without questioning it (Rojon and McDowall, 2010). In contrast, I have found these very traits in clients living in very individualist and horizontal cultures, such as the United States.

Is feedback equally effective in all cultures?

There is little research on the impact of culture on coach-to-client feedback. Coultas et al. (2011) concluded that in individualist cultures, people are more likely to respond well to one-on-one feedback while in collectivist cultures, they prefer group feedback. In cultures where shame is to be avoided and the concern for face is very high, people will not respond well to negative feedback. If a client comes from a feedback-adverse culture (which sometimes can be the very organization they work for), it is possible that they may not be willing to give you feedback. I encourage you to probe your client about the cultural values that underlie the effectiveness of feedback, before you decide to introduce the feedback protocol. Here are a few markers:

- Clients who live in collectivist cultures will prefer not to focus on you. As a result, they will most likely resist any invitation to single you out.
- Clients who live in power-distance cultures may see you as a mentor. Consequently, they will believe that it is not their place to give you feedback.
- Clients who live in face-saving cultures will refrain from giving any feedback they perceive as negative for fear of shaming you.

Once you have established that feedback is likely to be beneficial to the coaching process, that there is no foreseeable risk for the client, and feedback is clearly part of the contract, you are ready to start. The next chapter will introduce a protocol to do so.

Reflective questions about Chapter 7

How comfortable are you with the idea of contracting with your client for feedback?

What potential obstacles can you envision?

What are you planning to do to overcome them?

What are you prepared to experiment with?

What are your views about the influence of the client's cultures on the coaching process?

8 Collecting and using client feedback

Chapter summary

- Much can be learned from the implementation of client feedback protocols in other helping disciplines including psychotherapy, education, and
  sports coaching
- The client feedback protocol in executive coaching spans three sessions.
  It includes the administration of two sets of summative questions and
  one formative feedback scale, the EXCBOS, during the coaching session.
  During the intersession phase, the coach engages in reflective practice

Purpose of Chapter 8

This chapter proposes a structured protocol to collect and leverage client feedback
data in service of the professional development of the executive coach. It starts
with what can be learned from other disciplines. It then presents a protocol adapted
to executive coaching, concluding with a commented case study.

What can be learned from other helping disciplines

In this section of the chapter, I draw from a body of knowledge in other helping
disciplines which has informed the structure of the client feedback protocol adapted
to executive coaching.

Scope of the feedback

In Chapter 1, I established that a mixed-methods approach to client feedback was
suitable to support the professional development of the executive coach. This

meant that client feedback would be collected situationally in relation to a particular client and set of coaching sessions. This is aligned with the most recent student feedback protocol instruments developed in education (Gaertner, 2014) and sports coaching (Fletcher and Roberts, 2013). Indeed, these two disciplines combine formative and summative feedback in relation to either a particular teaching module or to a particular game. In mentoring, the collection of protégés' feedback is also based on a mixed-methods approach (Brodeur et al., 2015).

When to ask for feedback

Helping disciplines that have implemented client (or student) feedback request it at the end of the intervention. In sports coaching, athletes typically rate effective leadership behaviours of their sport coach right after an important game and discuss it together in relation to the result of the game (Chelladurai and Saleh, 1980; Fletcher and Roberts, 2013). In psychotherapy, summative feedback is requested both at the beginning of the session (and is related to the previous session) and at the end of the session (Miller et al., 2015). The advantage of starting with summative feedback at the beginning of the session is that it offers a baseline. For the executive coaching process, I suggest following the before/after principle for summative feedback, and to use formative feedback at the end of the coaching session.

Frequency of feedback

I could not find any study that has researched the ideal frequency of feedback. Psychotherapists collect feedback each session, sports coaches only after an important game, and educators at the end of a teaching module. Because executive coaching engagements vary greatly in their duration, I suggest getting feedback during three consecutive sessions and re-start if needed.

Reporting of the feedback results

The protocol I describe in this book is manual. However, there is clearly a potential to use a web interface, as is already done in other disciplines such as psychotherapy and education. I plan to develop an application downloadable to a mobile phone in the near future.

Use of client feedback data

The next chapter will focus on the use of client feedback in the supervision of coaches and the mentoring of student coaches. Here, I address the benefits of client feedback data on the quality of the reflective practice of the executive coach.

Reflective practice

As I mentioned in Chapter 3, reflection on self has been theorized as a process by which practitioners examine their behaviours, thoughts, feelings, and assumptions in relation to their coaching practice (Bachkirova, 2015). Schön (1984) distinguished between reflection-in-action and reflection-on-action. When 'in action', reflection consists in observing what we are thinking and doing in the moment; when 'on action', reflection involves stepping back and reflecting on a past event. Arguably, the client feedback protocol supports a reflection 'in action' at the beginning of the session and 'on action' after the session has ended.

Grant et al. (2002) argued that self-reflection in itself does not necessarily lead to clarity of understanding and could lead to rumination. In his view, what is more important is to achieve self-insight. Client feedback is likely to promote the transition from self-reflection to self-insight by adding one more element, deliberate practice.

Deliberate practice

When activated, self-insight leads to aspirational goals and experimentation, thus increasing the likelihood of sustained behavioural change (Hullinger et al., 2019). In multiple disciplines including sports and music, the best performers increase self-insight by developing domain-specific knowledge through a process of deliberate practice. It consists in three steps: having an accurate assessment of one's current level of performance, receiving on-going feedback on it, and rehearsing skills that need perfecting (Ericsson et al., 2006). The deliberate practitioner sets challenges that go beyond their current level of reliable achievement, in a safe learning context, that allows immediate feedback data and gradual refinement by repetition. Because the client feedback instrument collects detailed information about the prevalence of essential coaching skills and behaviours, it is ideally suited to support a process of deliberate practice.

Is client feedback useful for experienced coaches?

Feedback theory predicts that the level of professional development of the coach is likely to decrease the effectiveness of formative feedback. The coach-developmental theory has suggested that external feedback data, whether it comes from the client or from another source, might become less important as the coach matures professionally and is able to rely solely on internal feedback (Clutterbuck, 2010). Does it mean that the feedback instrument is more suitable for less experienced coaches?

Not according to theoreticians of deliberate practice in psychotherapy (Chow et al., 2015). Indeed, Ericsson et al. (2006) reject the claim that mastery consists in unconscious performance. On the contrary, masters need to regain control over the most difficult aspect of their practices and identify specific behaviours that they can improve on, by actively soliciting formative feedback from those who benefit from their craft.

The three-session protocol to solicit client feedback in executive coaching

Before you start

Time is scarce during an executive coaching session. As a result, the balance between the learning and development of the client and that of the coach must be managed. During the contracting phase, you'll need to investigate, based on what you understand about the espoused values of your client, whether requesting client feedback might hinder the coaching process, thus outweighing its benefits. If unsure, it's best to abstain.

In addition, expect a learning curve until you can seamlessly include client feedback within your coaching session. When I partnered with other executive coaches to experiment with the protocol, we all felt the need to start with a client with whom we had worked with before and with whom we had developed mutual trust. This gave us permission to experiment and refine the protocol over time.

An overview of the protocol

The protocol spans three coaching sessions, as illustrated in Figure 8. It can be repeated a few times with the same client or with another client, based on the unique development needs that you have identified for yourself. It can also be adjusted to your needs. For instance, one of the executive coaches who tested the protocol with several clients, instead of administrating the entire set of questions contained in the EXCBOS every time, focused on particular behaviours once he had detected an area of development.

The first session of the cycle

At the beginning of the session

The process begins by administering a set of questions that measure, retrospectively, the generation of new insights by the client during and after the previous coaching session. The questions assess the generation of new insights by focusing on the occurrence of 'aha' moments in coaching, during which serendipitous connections are made in the brain through an active dialogue with the coach, resulting in novel ideas or perspectives (Kets De Vries, 2013). Arguably, a retrospective assessment of cognitive change is more accurate than a pre-post comparison of the

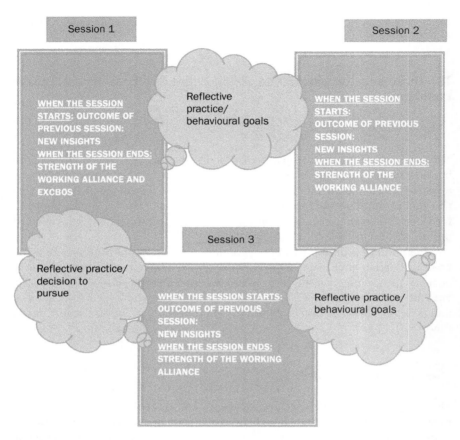

Figure 8   The three-session protocol to collect client feedback in executive coaching

same cognitive scale, such as, for example, an emotional intelligence test (Peterson, 1993). Indeed, successful coaching interventions may lead clients to experience transformational learning or gamma change which will shift the conceptualization of the cognitive scale between the time of the first and second measure (Ely et al., 2010). Let's take an example: before being coached, Susan took an emotional intelligence test and ranked herself largely above average on a measure of self-awareness. After the coaching engagement ends, she takes the same emotional intelligence test but this time ranks herself slightly below average on self-awareness. Does this mean that she is less self-aware as a result of the coaching? Not necessarily. An alternative explanation is that she now has a different perspective on the questions that comprise the test. She may be responding to the same questions but they have taken a new meaning for her. As a result, comparing her answers to the test pre- and post-coaching may be invalid.

Tip 1: Ask questions verbally

When I administer the client feedback protocol, my preference is to ask the questions verbally rather than giving a handout to the client. This allows me to stay in control of the process.

Tip 2: Maintain the pace

I also recommend going through the process quickly. Contract with the client ahead of time to limit any questions to a request for clarification during the administration process. While I stay open to the possibility that the client may bring additional inquiries or information that will nourish the coaching conversation, these are best dealt with after the survey has been completed.

Table 11 suggests a script to introduce the set of questions related to the generation of new insights experienced by the client during and after the last session. Table 12 displays the questions.

If you obtained a score of less than 3 for one or more of these questions, you might want to investigate further with your client. Doing so might act as a useful transition to the start of the coaching session. Possible inquires include:

- What do you make of your responses?
- How would you characterize your key takeaways from our last session?
- Any thoughts that might guide our discussion today?
- May I share my thoughts on your responses?

Table 11 Script to introduce the generation of new insights to the client

Before we start our session, I am going to ask you some questions to measure the extent to which you experienced new insights as a result of our last session. It is important that you don't hold back and are honest and candid with me. This will benefit our session today.

Remind yourself about the issues and topics you brought to our last coaching session. Thinking about what we discussed during the session and what you thought about after the session, listen to each assertion and tell me if you agree with it on a scale of 1 to 5, where 1 indicates that you agree with it to a limited extent and 5 to a great extent.

Table 12 Questions about the generation of new insights

A. I gained insights on the issues/topics we discussed

|———|———|———|———|
1   2   3   4   5

B. Some insights were unexpected and/or surprised me

|———|———|———|———|
1   2   3   4   5

C. I was able to recombine old ideas differently to create a new idea

|———|———|———|———|
1   2   3   4   5

D. I have new perspective(s) about the issues/topics I presented

|———|———|———|———|
1   2   3   4   5

E. I obtained more clarity about the issues/topics I presented

|———|———|———|———|
1   2   3   4   5

At the end of the session

At first, measure the strength of the working alliance using a set of questions that assess the level of bonding and agreement that the client believes exist between the two of you. Table 13 proposes a script to introduce these questions; Table 14 lists the questions.

Table 13 Script to introduce the working alliance to the client

Now that our session has ended, I am going to ask you some questions to measure how you experienced the quality of our working alliance today. It is important that you don't hold back and are honest and candid with me. This will benefit the quality of our work together going forward.

   Looking back at our session, listen to the following assertions and let me know if you agree with them. Rate 1 if you agree to a limited extent and 5 if you agree to a great extent.

Table 14 Questions related to the working alliance as experienced by your client

F. We agreed about how to proceed to discuss the issues/topics I presented

|———|———|———|———|
1   2   3   4   5

(continued)

Table 14 (continued)

G. We both felt that the coaching process was useful and productive

|—|—|—|—|
1   2   3   4   5

H. I believe that you appreciate me as a person

|—|—|—|—|
1   2   3   4   5

I. At times, I was not sure what we were trying to accomplish

|—|—|—|—|
5   4   3   2   1

J. I was confident in your ability to support me

|—|—|—|—|
1   2   3   4   5

K. We were aligned in our understanding of my coaching needs

|—|—|—|—|
1   2   3   4   5

L. We have a trusting working relationship

|—|—|—|—|
1   2   3   4   5

M. We can count on each other to achieve the coaching objective

|—|—|—|—|
1   2   3   4   5

N. Sometimes I felt that we had different ideas about my coaching need

|—|—|—|—|
5   4   3   2   1

Then, administer the EXCBOS. A script is proposed in Table 15, while Table 16 provides the list of questions.

Table 15 Script to introduce the EXCBOS to the client

Now, I am going to ask you some questions about specific executive coaching behaviours I may have engaged in and you might have observed during the coaching session. Again, it is important that you don't hold back and are honest and candid with me. This will benefit the quality of our work together going forward.

Looking back at our session today, I am going to share a number of statements concerning my own behaviours during the coaching session. Let me know to what extent you agree with these statements. A score of 1 means that you agree to a very limited extent and a score of 6 that you agree to a great extent.

Table 16 Questions contained in the EXCBOS

O. I remained open-minded to what you said

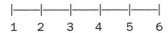

P. I remained non-judgemental

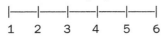

Q. When you presented an issue, I neither over-reacted nor stayed overly neutral

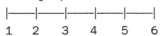

R. I was responsive to your needs

S. I acknowledged your emotions when discussing a topic

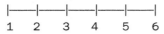

T. I communicated authentically, transparently, honestly

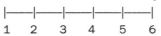

U. I was supportive

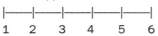

V. I showed positive regard

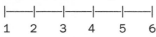

W. I checked whether my understanding of your organization was sufficient to discuss the issues you presented

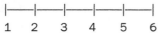

X. I invited you to explore how you typically approach change

Y. I asked you questions about your organization to better understand the issues you presented

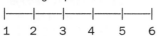

(continued)

Table 16   (continued)

Z.   I used examples from coaching engagements in other organizations to broaden your perspective on a situation

```
|——|——|——|——|——|
1    2    3    4    5    6
```

AA. When shifting from inquiry to advisory mode, I made this explicit to you

```
|——|——|——|——|——|
1    2    3    4    5    6
```

AB. When you requested advice, I checked first if this was what you really needed and then invited you to reflect on your request

```
|——|——|——|——|——|
1    2    3    4    5    6
```

AC. I invited you to explore unintended consequences of your actions

```
|——|——|——|——|——|
1    2    3    4    5    6
```

AD. I used examples from my own life story to illustrate a point you made

```
|——|——|——|——|——|
1    2    3    4    5    6
```

AE. I invited you to reflect on the alignment between your goals and the goals of your organization

```
|——|——|——|——|——|
1    2    3    4    5    6
```

AF. I invited you to state your personal vision for your role in your organization

```
|——|——|——|——|——|
1    2    3    4    5    6
```

AG. I invited you to reflect on whether your organization's culture enables or hampers your development goals

```
|——|——|——|——|——|
1    2    3    4    5    6
```

AH. When you expressed concerns about confidentiality, I invited you to discuss these concerns

```
|——|——|——|——|——|
1    2    3    4    5    6
```

AI. When unable to provide expertise, I acknowledged the fact

```
|——|——|——|——|——|
1    2    3    4    5    6
```

After thanking the client for their response, you might want to reiterate that you are looking forward to using their feedback to further your development as a practitioner. Remind the client that you intend to ask for feedback at the start and at the end of the next two sessions, and ask them if they are comfortable with that.

Tip 3: What if the client says that you did not display a behaviour because it was not needed?

I suggest you score yourself a 1 and make a note on the side. After the session, you will have a chance to reflect further about the relevance of the behaviour during this particular coaching session.

Tip 4: Strategies for time management

The EXCBOS is a long survey that is administrated at the end of the first coaching session in the cycle. What if you run out of time?

Testing the protocol with a few clients who already have a trusting relationship with you will allow you to experiment and explore with approaches that work for you. Here are some suggestions from executive coaches who have used the protocol.

Ask questions O to V at the end of the first session of the cycle (which focus on empathic behaviours) and questions W to AI at the end of the second session of the cycle (which focus on the transformational learning behaviours).

As you come to understand your strengths and development areas further, you might want to use the EXCBOS as a menu, focusing on a particular cluster of behaviours. The important thing is never to become complacent: don't necessarily focus on behaviours that warrant development. Sometimes, it's good to revisit behaviours that relate to your strengths.

Between the first and second session of the cycle

Immediately after the first session, make a note of your immediate reaction to the client scores on the working alliance.

- Are you surprised by some of the scores?
- If you had been asked the same questions, how would you have responded?

Calculate your score on empathy on the EXCBOS

- Cognitive Empathy (CE): average of O + P + Q
- Sharing Empathy (SE): average of R + S
- Nurturing Empathy (NE): average of T + U + V
- TOTAL EMPATHY: average of CE + SE + NE

If you obtained less than 4.9 on average, your score is below that of 80% of the coaches who participated in the research.

Calculate your score on transformational learning on the EXCBOS

- Preparation (PR): average of W + X + Y
- Creativity (CR): average of Z + AA + AB + AC + AD
- Goal Alignment (GO): average of AE + AF + AG
- Managing Ruptures of Trust (MA): average of AH + AI
- TOTAL TRANSFORMATION: average of PR + CR + GO + MA

If you obtained less than 3.8 on average, your score is below that of 80% of the coaches who participated in the research.

Engage in reflective and deliberate practice

- Set aside time to reflect about your reactions to your scores on the two sets of questions concerning the coaching outcome: those concerning the generation of new insights and those concerning the strength of the working alliance. If you are surprised by your scores, ask yourself if it could be related to any of your scores in the EXCBOS. Indeed, my research showed that scores on the EXCBOS were related to measures of the strength of the working alliance on the one hand, and the generation of new insights for the client on the other.
- Examine your scores on each behaviour on the EXCBOS, paying attention to low scores. As I mentioned above, sometimes a low score may signify that the behaviour was simply not needed. For example, if you have coached other clients in the same organization, you might not need behaviour Y (I asked you questions about your organization to better understand the issues you presented). If you believe that the session did not warrant the particular behaviour, consider administering the EXCBOS again at the next session.
- Then pay attention to your average score on the components (for example, empathy) or facets of the components (for example, creativity). If your average score is lower than what 80% of the coaches achieved in the research, reflect about what you could do differently in future sessions.

- Practise some of your lower-scoring behaviours with other clients.
- Seek guidance (from your supervisor, peers, through research, literature, etc.) on how to improve as needed.
- Set behavioural goals for yourself and be intentional as you prepare for upcoming coaching sessions with your client.

During and in between the second and third sessions in the cycle

- Ask the insight-generation questions (A to E) at the start of the session and the questions about the strength of the working alliance (F to N) at the end of the session.
- If the client was not able to rate you on 5 behaviours or more in the last session (because they were not needed), consider administering the EXC-BOS again.
- Engage in reflective and deliberate practice as described above.
- Compare your results with those of the first session. Do you note a change? Can you make a link between some of the behavioural adjustments you consciously made and changes in your scores?

After the third and final session of the cycle

Consider whether engaging in a second cycle of feedback with the same client is relevant by checking if:

- You continue to score in the low range for some behaviours, facets or components
- There was no change in your scores, or they decreased during the cycle
- You have consciously changed some of your behaviours but you are not clear on how this has impacted your scores.

If you have answered 'yes' to one or more of these questions, I suggest that you discuss with your client about what has worked and not worked for you so far. Here are some possible questions:

- What do you wish you had told me during our last session?
- What would make you get more from our session today?
- What would you like to focus on or discuss more (or less) during our session today?
- What else occurs to you to make the coaching more effective?

Based on their response, use your own judgement to decide whether or not it makes sense to continue a second cycle. If this feels impractical, consider starting a new cycle with another client.

Case study

Tom recently started coaching Jane, a VP of Supply Chain in an international consumer product company. Jane has established a clear coaching need: she would like to develop her self-confidence and assertiveness, so that her voice can be better heard in the executive team to which she belongs. Tom has obtained agreement from both Jane and her sponsor, the VP of HR, to use the client feedback protocol. Because Jane is familiar with executive coaching, they both agree to start using the feedback instrument during the second coaching session. At the beginning of the session, Tom asks questions about the generation of new insights. He obtains straight 5s. Jane indicates her interest in exploring the meaning of the scores, because she would like to be viewed as more creative by her supervisor and her peers during the executive team meetings.

Tom: So, Jane, what do you make of your responses to the survey?

Jane: What I experienced was that you gave me a lot of space to think during the first session, and that you challenged me to get out of my own head and to stop making hypotheses about what others might think. This forced me to consider multiple possible scenarios about the pros and cons of me speaking up during my boss's team meetings. This is food for thought for me. I want to do the same in the executive meetings.

Tom: Would you like to explore this further?

Jane: No, it's clear to me what I need to do more.

Tom: OK. So, how would you characterize your key takeaways from the last session?

Jane: That I have to understand the perspective of my peers better, their needs, and also my boss's needs, before making assumptions about what they might think about my contributions. It almost makes me feel like I was selfish! Only considering my own needs ... fears ... instead of tuning in to others!

Tom: Any thoughts that might guide our discussion today?

Jane: Yeah, I need to find the courage to speak up. I am not quite sure how to achieve this.

Tom: May I share my thoughts on your responses?

Jane: Sure!

Tom: Well basically it's a thought about what you just said. As you think of yourself not being courageous enough, I am reminded of something you shared with me during our first session, that when you are well prepared, you have the most important facts in place, you never have a problem speaking up. I wonder if we could explore this strength further during our session today, as a starting point to explore the theme of courage? Thoughts?

Notice how Tom used the questions he asks to Jane about her new insights to kick-off the session. The questions eased very well into an exploration of the learning that has taken place for the client between the two sessions. It also allowed the client to transition to a presenting issue.

The case study continued ...

The session proceeds and arrives at a natural ending about 5 minutes ahead of schedule. Tom asks Jane if she feels complete for today. Jane's response is positive and Tom then asks whether Jane is ready to go through the rest of the feedback protocol as a conclusion to the session. He reiterates that he will use Jane's feedback to reflect on how he can be even more effective as a coach and that the information will be used by him alone. Jane agrees and Tom first asks questions about her perspective on the strength of the working alliance, and then administers the EXCBOS.

At the end of the session, Tom notices that he scored 4s and 5s on the working alliance questions, something he expected. Indeed, the mutual trust and level of agreement have been generally strong with Jane since the very beginning of the coaching process. He gets an almost perfect score of 5.9 on empathic behaviours, which again does not surprise him. While Tom's average score on transformational learning behaviours is 4.9, there are a few behaviours where he scored 3 or lower. He wants to reflect more about the scores that he obtained on the following behaviours:

- I used examples from coaching engagements in other organizations to broaden your perspective on a situation
- I used examples from my own life story to illustrate a point you made
- I invited you to reflect on whether your organization's culture enables or hampers your development goals
- When unable to provide expertise, I acknowledged the fact

Tom starts by reflecting about the relevance of these behaviours during this second coaching session. Could it be that there were no opportunities to use them? He finds this was not the case. Tom is familiar with the concept of parallel process, and starts to reflect whether the lack of courage that Jane has explored during the coaching session has somehow transferred to him. Tom reflects that Jane's supervisor and her peers tend to behave and decide in a forceful manner, while she has a steadier and more subdued approach. While it is clear to Tom that Jane has a unique style, which benefits the team's decision quality, there is an expectation that all team members conform to traditional male behaviours. Over the years, Tom coached a few female leaders who never quite found their voice in a male-dominated executive team. Somehow, Tom realizes that he felt personally guilty about the outcome each time, and had never properly processed the emotion. He understands that he is making an assumption that by not asking Jane questions that leverage his former experience, he will avoid feeling guilty. The reality is that he is trying to help himself instead of helping Jane. Tom considers the possibility of conducting a one-off experiment, consisting in telling Jane the story of one of her former clients (obviously by changing names and context to ensure confidentiality) and invite her to reflect how she could have helped this particular client.

Note how the feedback received by Tom on the strength of the working alliance and the EXCBOS lead him to reflect on his capabilities rather than on his skills. It also opened up the possibility of new coaching interventions.

What do you make of this? What ratings do you think you would have received from the last session you completed? What avenues of inquiry does this lead to?

Concluding thoughts

According to the executive coaches who have used the feedback protocol, its administration did not compromise the flow of the coaching sessions. Their clients have been intrigued and encouraged by the coaches' willingness to continue developing themselves by asking them for feedback. They understood the process and responded to the questions effectively, and it did not hamper the logistics of the coaching.

However, the most difficult part was the reflective process, especially when the scores were not what they had expected. Psychotherapy research tells us that receiving negative feedback (especially at the start of an intervention) is actually a sign that the client is engaged. Best-in-class therapists tend to receive negative feedback early, address it, and then consistently score higher. Less effective therapists receive average feedback early, but the trend is downwards and the clients drop out more often. The difference is that best-in-class practitioners work very hard and engage in deliberate practice early during an intervention to address any gap. This can be very difficult and it is not always possible to make the reflective journey alone. The next chapter will discuss the role that mentors and supervisors of executive coaches can play to support the reflective practice of the executive coach.

Reflective questions about Chapter 8

What was your emotional state coming into this chapter and what it is now?

What do you make of this?

What else have you discovered about your attitude to client feedback?

What questions remain?

What are you prepared to do differently in your practice?

9   Using client feedback in supervision and mentoring

Chapter summary

- Several models of mentoring and supervision in coaching encourage the exploration of the client perspective, but do not use feedback data from them
- Two issues deserve attention: managing the self-deception of the coach and adapting the use of the client feedback protocol to their level of experience
- The Johari Window is suggested as an entry point to examine client feedback data in supervision and mentoring

Purpose of Chapter 9

Drawing from research and my own experience as a supervisor and mentor of executive coaches, this chapter makes the case that client feedback data can strengthen the supervision and mentoring of coaches, from student to experienced practitioner.

Definition and functions of supervision and mentoring

There are multiple definitions of supervision and mentoring in coaching, and they sometimes overlap. As a result, I introduce the chapter with my working definition of supervision grounded in a review of the literature.

Supervision of coaches

The International Coach Federation (ICF) published the following definition of supervision in February 2020: 'a collaborative learning practice to continually build the capacity of the coach through reflective dialogue for the benefit of both coaches and clients' (ICF, 2020a).

In 2019, as the co-chair of the research committee of the Graduate School Alliance for Education in Coaching (GSAEC), I co-led a project to update their knowledge base on supervision. Based on a thorough review of the literature, we recognized that supervision supports a variety of learning objectives for the coach, including increasing their domain knowledge, their fluency navigating the coaching assignment as a complex adaptive system, their skill base, their cognitive development, their professional identity, and their ethical maturity. Arguably, supervisors use external feedback data to support a developmental conversation with the coach. Consequently, they activate the coach's internal feedback system by inviting them to reflect on the different perspectives present within the coaching system they operate in.

Mentoring for accreditation

The role of the mentor is narrower than that of the supervisor, as it is generally focused on supporting the acquisition of knowledge and skills. The ICF defines mentor coaching as the provision of 'professional assistance in achieving and demonstrating the levels of coaching competency demanded by the desired credential level sought by a coach-applicant (mentee)' (2020b). As part of their role, mentors are often expected to provide feedback on tapes of coaching sessions submitted by the student.

Mentoring within a coach training programme

The role of the mentor of coaches studying towards a certificate or graduate degree is similar to that of a mentor in accreditation. Their mission is to prepare the student for an oral exam that assesses their skill set against an accrediting standard. In such capacity, mentors are expected to provide feedback either on live coaching sessions (involving fellow students) or on recorded client sessions provided by the student.

The case for using client feedback data in supervision and mentoring

Several models of coaching supervision promote the exploration of the client's perspective. For example, the Gestalt model recognizes the client as an 'absent presence' and invites the coach to reflect on the interactions between the field of the coach–client relationship and the field of the client system. The cognitive behavioural approach of supervision encourages coaches and supervisors to listen to clients' tapes or transcripts. The transactional analysis approach seeks to uncover to what extent the coach and the client are psychologically close. Finally, the social models – such as the Seven-eyed model (Hawkins and Smith, 2013) – consider the client's system, the coach–client relationship, and the wider context in which both the client and the coach work together.

However, the collection of feedback data direct from the client has not been encouraged, nor its effects researched in the context of supervision or mentoring. As I argued in Chapter 3, there is a real danger of not including direct client feedback data in any professional development discussion for the coach, since clients offer a unique and at times complementary perspective to that of external observers.

Findings from psychotherapy research (Reese et al., 2009) suggest that the injection of client feedback data during the supervision process may have multiple beneficial effects, including:

- Helping therapists focus on clients whose feedback is problematic and may benefit the most from being discussed in supervision.
- Helping supervisors focus on clients whose feedback is consistently positive, thus supporting a strength-based approach; this is likely to trigger the therapist's resourcefulness with problematic clients.
- Balancing the subjective view of the supervisor and the therapist with that of the client.
- Reaching better outcomes with clients. Such an effect was measured empirically in one study (Reese et al., 2009), by demonstrating that the outcomes of clients counselled by therapists using supervision with client feedback were superior to the outcomes of clients counselled by therapists using supervision without client feedback.
- Offering both to the supervisor and the therapist a way to complement or replace the listening to client tapes when those are not available.
- Giving permission to the supervisor to be more balanced between the use of positive and negative feedback without decreasing the strength of the working alliance with the therapist.

Addressing the resistance of the coach

In Chapter 3, I recognized that coaches are unlikely to trust their clients as a relevant source of feedback because they generally do not see them as credible (Atkinson and Butcher, 2003). Not only are they unlikely to solicit client feedback, but when they receive unsolicited feedback, it is unlikely to influence their future behaviours. The client feedback instrument, because it has been empirically developed, can then be used in a pragmatic way as a starting point for a dialogue. As such it places the feedback process firmly within the wisdom of the client–coach relationship instead of within the client's individual knowledge, thus offering a more trustworthy platform for the coach.

However, a more formidable barrier may impact the effectiveness of the client feedback protocol: the performance anxiety of the coach. Bachkirova (2015) has suggested that receiving negative feedback from a client is conflated with the fear of rejection. Negative self-assessments that result from such fears are amplified in the expert's discourse, which states that the coach is solely responsible to choose the 'right' technique and drive the success of the intervention. The problem is that the fear of rejection is a major trigger of self-deception for the coach. Once self-deception is in place, it feeds the tendency to block new information, such as client feedback, initiating a vicious cycle (Ditto and Lopez, 1992). While supervision or mentoring might be a way to counter a fear of rejection, Bachkirova remarked that if the coach is in the grip of self-deception, 'the relevant material may not reach supervision at all' (2015: 5). To address this obstacle, I invite coaches and their mentors or supervisors to discuss the coach's general attitudes to feedback prior to soliciting it. By addressing their resistance to client feedback ahead of initiating the process, coaches may improve their listening skills and their capacity to internalize the information received from their clients. Arguably, longitudinal studies of the benefits of student feedback in education and sports coaching indicate that such internalization is clearly at work, since self-assessments made by teachers and assessment provided by students converge over time (Gaertner, 2014).

Potential issues with student coaches

In the previous chapter, I made the case that executive coaches whose experience may have facilitated the alignment between their self-evaluations and those of their clients can still benefit from client feedback if they engage in deliberate practice. At the other end of the professional development spectrum, feedback research suggests that students or beginner coaches are more likely to accept client feedback and consider them as equal because of their inexperience. However, when I presented the EXCBOS to coach educators, they indicated that some of the behaviours contained in the instrument are more likely to be present at later stages of the coach's professional development journey. For example, the fact that most behaviours are presented in a collaborative language refer to the co-creation of the coaching process with the client. Such behaviours may require an eclectic approach to coaching which typically emerges after several years of practice. Likewise, newly trained coaches may first need to put the emphasis on powerful questioning so that they can definitely let go of their tendency to overuse advice. While this may at first hamper the creativity phase of the transformational learning process in coaching, it may be necessary so that novice coaches rehearse and internalize inquiry-based behaviours. As a result, I invite educators to discuss and select relevant behaviours with students when using the EXCBOS.

Using client feedback data in supervision and mentoring

The Johari Window (Luft and Ingham, 1961) was originally developed to raise one's self-awareness about interpersonal behaviours. It has been reformulated to apply

Quadrant 1: **Unacknowledged Strength** I am pleasantly surprised with my high score	Quadrant 2: **Confirmed Strength** I was expecting the high score I received
Quadrant 4: **Blind Spot** I am disappointed with my low score	Quadrant 3: **Confirmed Development Opportunity** I was expecting the low score I received

Figure 9   Adaptation of the Johari Window to client feedback data

to a wide variety of learning situations, including in psychotherapy and education (Halpern, 2009). In addition, it is often used by executive coaches to support the interpretation of a multi-rater feedback instrument by their clients (Maxwell, 2016).

Building on these applications, I suggest using the Johari Window to support a conversation about the EXCBOS in the mentoring or supervision space. The first step is to eliminate the behaviours which were not relevant to the particular coaching situation. Once this has been done, the coach places the remaining behaviours in each quadrant based on their reaction to each score, as indicated in Figure 9.

Several models of supervision support the exploration of the window. I introduce a few models in this chapter and encourage coaches, supervisors, and mentors to consider the applicability of their preferred models to the exploration of the Johari Window.

Discounting

Discounting happens when the coach ignores or minimizes events that have happened during a coaching session. It is a protective device to keep the coach's frame of reference intact and may be useful in certain situations. It can backfire if the coach's world map clashes with the client's expectations and needs (Hay, 2007).

Discounting of a situation and of its significance

In the 'blind spot' quadrant, there is a possibility that the coach may have discounted a client need that warranted a coaching behaviour(s) that was not sufficiently displayed. Alternatively, while having recognized the client need, the coach may have discounted its significance and as a result failed to display the warranted coaching behaviour(s).

The following set of questions will help the coach become more self-aware and reconnect with the underlying needs of the client:

- What was happening?
- Who was saying and doing what?

- What expressions/gestures were there?
- What does this mean?
- How is this an issue or problem?

Working with higher levels of discounting

With behaviours in the 'confirmed development opportunity' quadrant, we are dealing with a coach who is self-aware but might lack resourcefulness. The supervisor and mentor can suggest an exploration of the three levels of the discounting model, inviting the coach to consider whether:

- there is a possible solution to become more fluent with the behaviour(s)
- the coach has or can acquire the skills to do so
- there is a plan to improve

If the coach is resourceful but still blocked, the supervisor may need to work at the sixth level of the model, exploring with the coach whether there is a hidden assumption that there are benefits of taking no action. A discussion about competing commitments that block action may be needed (Kegan and Lahey, 2001).

Gestalt

Gestalt promotes moment-to-moment awareness of our experience of self and of the external world, and encourages us to notice where we might have experienced blockages. The process facilitates creative adjustment to changes in our environment (Greenberg, 1980).

The chair exercise is probably one of the best-known techniques to trigger awareness. It is suitable to explore quadrant 3 ('confirmed development opportunity') or quadrant 4 ('blind spot'). In the first chair, the coach reflects as the coach and in the second chair as a client.

In the first chair, as a coach, reflective questions include:

- My way of being during the session:
  - What was the quality of my listening?
  - What was my emotional state when I entered in the conversation? Is there a chance it might be acting as a filter on my listening or understanding?
  - What assumptions was I making? How might these be acting as a filter on my listening and my understanding?
- How I helped:
  - What did I do to enhance the quality of the client's thinking?
  - Was I appropriately directive or non-directive?
  - Did we go too fast in moving to action?

- What choices I made:
  - What questions did I withhold and why?
  - Was I sufficiently challenging?
  - Did I give the client sufficient time to think?
- What I learned
  - What patterns can I discern from this and previous conversations with this client?
  - What would I do differently another time?
  - What requests would I like to make to my client?
- What are my concerns
  - Where did I struggle?
  - What negative emotions am I aware of?

In the second chair, as a client, reflective questions include:

- What was the client saying and not saying?
- What was quality of the client's thinking?
- What had the client learned from the previous session?
- How had the client's perceptions changed?
- What issues had been resolved and what new issues had arisen?
- What topics did the client want to bring to the conversation?
- What was the client's motivation for bringing these topics?
- How prepared was the client to be challenged?
- What did the client do to support me? What worked and what did not work?

Strength-based conversation

The purpose of a strength-based conversation is to enhance awareness of our strengths and our resourcefulness to use them to address a particular issue (Aguinis et al., 2012).

It is a useful tool to discuss both quadrant 1 ('unacknowledged strength') and quadrant 2 ('confirmed strength') in the Johari Window. Here are a proposed set of questions to lead the reflection:

1. Think back over your experience as a coach, and remember an especially satisfying accomplishment in which your contribution was appreciated.
   - Without being humble, what do you most value about your skills, talents, and strengths that you bring to your work?
   - What positive feedback have you received about your strengths that has helped you validate your talents?
2. Looking back at your feedback results, where do you see your strengths at play? And where do you not see them at play?
3. Think of a time when someone helped you identify and build one of your strengths:

   o   What did the other person do that was successful in helping you
       develop?
   o   What was the impact on you?
4. What activities have been most useful in helping you develop those
    strengths?
5. What advice would you give to me for further developing your strengths in
    the context of our work? What on-the-job learning opportunities would I
    promote?

At another level, the strength-based conversation can address discounting issues
relevant to quadrant 3: 'confirmed development opportunities'. The following inquiries are suggested:

*   Which of your current strengths are transferable?
*   How could you use existing strengths to experiment with these behaviours?
*   What would learning look like from a place of strength?
*   What requests could you make to your client or other stakeholder to sup-
    port you?

Enhancing the supervision or mentoring space

In this chapter, I have made the case for and proposed strategies to leverage client
feedback data in a supervision or mentoring session. Arguably the same techniques
can be used to leverage any other source of external feedback received by the
coach such as data from peers, other mentors or supervisors, external observers,
and assessors.

This presents an interesting proposition for supervisors and mentors. In parallel with the dominant discourse placing the coach on a pedestal of expertise and the
client on the receiving end, it could be argued that supervisors or mentors are sometimes placed on a pedestal by coaches. Bandura's theory of social-cognitive feedback (1977) predicts that the supervisor, because of their professional credibility
and knowledge, are much more likely to influence the coach's self-efficacy through
their feedback than other sources.

The injection of client feedback data, alongside other sources of feedback
data, may help rebalance the relationship between the supervisor or mentor and the
coach, in the same way that it rebalances the relationship between the coach and
the client. On that basis, the supervision or mentoring space can be viewed as a hub
where complementary sources of feedback interact in service of the professional
development of the executive coach.

Reflective questions about Chapter 9

On scale of 1 to 5, where 1 = 'not likely', how likely are you to use or request the use of direct client feedback data in supervision and mentoring?

If you are a 1 or a 2, use the discounting model or the chair exercise to explore your objections to using client feedback data.

Parting words

As I finalize this chapter, it's been almost a year since the Covid-19 pandemic began. The structure of my working day may not have changed much: my practice is now 100% online instead of 75%. But the substance of the coaching conversations has evolved profoundly. For the majority of my clients, their world has been turned upside-down: they expect me to adapt with them.

It is very unlikely that the situation will have returned to normal by the time you read this book. While it is still early days as I write these lines, there is a sense that fundamental shifts are going to happen in the industries and companies that employ the executives we serve. For example, our clients will likely be asked to focus more on developing their human capabilities than their leadership competencies. The two components of the EXCBOS, empathy and transformational learning, allow executive coaches to support their clients as they navigate these shifts. I encourage you to hone those processes and the coaching capabilities that underlie them by getting started with client developmental feedback in your practice.

Engaging in client feedback may also support the growth of your practice. Last week I listened to an informative podcast about the need for executive coaches to rebrand themselves in the time of Covid-19. They reminded the listeners to start by revisiting the vision they have defined for their practice in the 'new normal'. What better way to do this than to tune in to what your clients have to say about how you impact them?

As you become familiar with the protocol and consider how to get started with client feedback, here is how you can start using the EXCBOS right now:

- Acknowledge the wisdom of your clients and build their credibility in your eyes, by making connections between the coaching behaviours contained in the EXCBOS and the leadership behaviours that your clients typically report using in their role.
- Reverse-engineer the summative feedback you have recently received from clients over the last few months by using the list of behaviours contained in the EXCBOS.
- When you start a new coaching engagement, get in the habit of promoting mutual transparency and declare that you will be explicit about the coaching tools and techniques that you are planning to use. Indeed, declarations are one of the most effective self-influencing techniques.
- Start using the client feedback protocol with clients you know well.
- Discuss this book with your peers, supervisors, and mentors.

All the best on your journey!

References

Aguinis, H., Gottfredson, R.K. and Joo, H. (2012) Delivering effective performance feedback: The strengths-based approach, *Business Horizons*, 55 (2): 105–111.

Anseel, F., Beatty, A.S., Shen, W., Lievens, F. and Sacket, P.R. (2015) How are we doing after 30 years? A meta-analytic review of the antecedents and outcomes of feedback-seeking behaviour, *Journal of Management*, 41 (1): 318–348.

Asay, T.P. and Lambert, M.J. (1999) The empirical case for the common factors in therapy: Quantitative findings, in M.A. Hubble, B.L. Duncan and S.D. Miller (eds.) *The Heart and Soul of Change: What works in therapy*, 23–55, Washington, DC: American Psychological Association.

Atkinson, S. and Butcher, D. (2003) Trust in managerial relationships, *Journal of Managerial Psychology*, 18 (4): 282–304.

Bachelor, A. (1988) How clients perceive therapist empathy: A content analysis of received empathy, *Psychotherapy: Theory, Research, Practice and Training*, 25 (2): 227–240.

Bachelor, A. (2013) Clients' and therapists' views of the therapeutic alliance: Similarities, differences and relationship to therapy outcome, *Clinical Psychology and Psychotherapy*, 20 (2): 118–135.

Bachkirova, T. (2011) *Developmental Coaching: Working with the self*, Maidenhead: Open University Press.

Bachkirova, T. (2015) Self-deception in coaches: An issue in principle and a challenge for supervision, *Coaching: An International Journal of Theory, Research and Practice*, 8 (1): 4–19.

Bachkirova, T. (2016) The self of the coach: Conceptualisation, issues, and opportunities for practitioner development, *Consulting Psychology Journal: Practice and Research*, 68 (2): 143–156.

Bachkirova, T., Arthur, L. and Reading, E. (2015) Evaluating a coaching and mentoring programme: Challenges and solutions, *International Coaching Psychology Review*, 10 (2): 175–189.

Bachkirova, T. and Borrington, S. (2019) Old wine in new bottles: Exploring pragmatism as a philosophical framework for the discipline of coaching, *Academy of Management Learning and Education*, 18 (3): 337–360.

Bachkirova, T., Jackson, P.M. and Clutterbuck, D. (2011) *Coaching and Mentoring Supervision: Theory and practice*, Maidenhead: Open University Press.

Bachkirova, T. and Lawton Smith, C. (2015) From competencies to capabilities in the assessment and accreditation of coaches, *International Journal of Evidence Based Coaching and Mentoring*, 13 (2): 123–140.

Backus, C.R. (2018) *The nature of the learning experiences of leadership coaches that lead to coaching competencies: A phenomenological study*, Dissertation, Washington, DC: George Washington University.

Bailey, C. and Fletcher, C. (2002) The impact of multiple source feedback on management development: Findings from a longitudinal study, *Journal of Organizational Behavior*, 23 (7): 853–867.

Bandura, A. (1977) Self-efficacy: Toward a unifying theory of behavioral change, *Psychological Review*, 84 (2): 191–215.

Baron, L. and Morin, L. (2009) The coach–coachee relationship in executive coaching: A field study, *Human Resource Development Quarterly*, 20 (1): 85-106.

Bartlett, J.E., II, Boylan, R.V. and Hale, J.E. (2014) Executive coaching: An integrative literature review, *Journal of Human Resource and Sustainability Studies*, 2 (4): 188–195.

Bennett, J.L. and Bush, M. (2014) *Coaching for Change*, New York: Routledge.

Birnie, J. (2019) Client-led coaching? First-time coaching clients' experience, *International Journal of Evidence Based Coaching and Mentoring*, S13: 102–113.

Blackman, A. (2006) Factors that contribute to the effectiveness of business coaching: The coachees' perspective, *Business Review, Cambridge*, 5 (1): 98–104.

Blackman, A., Moscardo, G. and Gray, D.E. (2016) Challenges for the theory and practice of business coaching: A systematic review of empirical evidence, *Human Resource Development Review*, 15 (4): 459–486.

Blumberg, K.M. (2014) Executive coaching competencies: A review and critique with implications for coach education, *Journal of. Psychological Issues in Organizational Culture*, 5 (2): 87–97.

Bono, J.E., Purvanova, R.K., Towler, A.J. and Peterson, D.B. (2009) A survey of executive coaching practices, *Personnel Psychology*, 62 (2): 361–404.

Bordin, E.S. (1979) The generalisability of the psychoanalytic concept of the working alliance, *Psychotherapy: Theory, Research and Practice*, 6 (3): 252–260.

Boston, J. (2013) *An Investigation into the Role of Client Feedback during the Coaching Process*, Henley-on-Thames: Henley Business School.

Boyatzis, R.E. (2006) An overview of intentional change from a complexity perspective, *Journal of Management Development*, 25 (7): 607–623.

Boyatzis, R.E. and Howard, A. (2015) When goal setting helps and hinders sustained, desired change, in S. David, D. Clutterbuck and D. Megginson (eds.) *Beyond Goals: Effective strategies for coaching and mentoring*, 211–228, Abingdon: Routledge.

Bozer, G., Joo, B.-K. and Santora, J.C. (2015) Executive coaching: Does coach–coachee matching based on similarity really matter?, *Consulting Psychology Journal: Practice and Research*, 67 (3): 218–233.

Bozer, G., Sarros, J.C. and Santora, J.C. (2013) The role of coachee characteristics in executive coaching for effective sustainability, *Journal of Management Development*, 32 (3): 277–294.

Bozer, G., Sarros, J.C. and Santora, J.C. (2014) Academic background and credibility in executive coaching effectiveness, *Personnel Review*, 43 (6): 881–897.

Braddick, C. (2010) *More process, less insight?* Available at: http://www.carolbraddick.com/pdf/MoreProcess_LessInsight_Oct2010.pdf [accessed: 28 November 2017].

Bright, M. (2015) *Working Towards a Tool to Help Define the Roles of an Executive Coach*, London: Middlesex University.

Brodeur, P., Larose, S., Tarabulsy, G., Feng, B., Forget-Dubois, N.J.M. and Learning, T.P.I. (2015) Development and construct validation of the mentor behavior scale, *Mentoring and Tutoring: Partnership in Learning*, 23 (1): 54–75.

Cadle, A.W. (2012) *The relationship between rating scales used to evaluate tasks from task inventories for licensure and certification examinations*, Unpublished DPhil dissertation, Tampa, FL: University of South Florida.

Cappelli, P. and Tavis, A. (2018) HR goes agile, *Harvard Business Review*, March/April. Available at: https://hbr.org/2018/03/the-new-rules-of-talent-management#hr-goes-agile.

Cavanagh, M. and Lane, D. (2012) Coaching psychology coming of age: The challenges we face in the messy world of complexity, *International Coaching Psychology Review*, 7 (1): 75–90.

Chelladurai, P. and Saleh, S.D. (1980) Dimensions of leader behavior in sports: Development of a leadership scale, *Journal of Sport Psychology*, 2 (1): 34–45.

Chow, D., Miller, S., Seidel, J., Kane, R.T., Thornton, J.A. and Andrews, W.P. (2015) The role of deliberate practice in the development of highly effective psychotherapists, *Psychotherapy*, 52 (3): 337–345.

Clemence, A.J., Hilsenroth, M.J., Ackerman, S.J., Strassle, C.G. and Handler, L. (2005) Facets of the therapeutic alliance and perceived progress in psychotherapy: Relationship between patient and therapist perspectives, *Clinical Psychology and Psychotherapy*, 12 (6): 443–454.

Clutterbuck, D. (2010) Coaching reflection: The liberated coach, *Coaching: An International Journal of Theory, Research and Practice*, 3 (1): 73–81.

Clutterbuck, D. and Spence, G. (2016) Working with goals in coaching, in T. Bachkirova, G. Spence and D. Drake (eds.) *The SAGE Handbook of Coaching*, 221–239, London: Sage.

Corbière, M., Bisson, J., Lauzon, S. and Ricard, N. (2006) Factorial validation of a French short-form of the Working Alliance Inventory, *International Journal of Methods in Psychiatric Research*, 15 (1): 36–45.

Coultas, C.W., Bedwell, W.L., Burke, C.S. and Salas, E. (2011) Values sensitive coaching: The delta approach to coaching culturally diverse executives, *Consulting Psychology Journal: Practice and Research*, 63 (3): 149–161.

Cox, E. (2013) *Coaching Understood: A pragmatic inquiry into the coaching process*, London: Sage.

Cox, E. (2015) Coaching and adult learning: Theory and practice, *New Directions for Adult and Continuing Education*, 2015 (148): 27–38.

Cox, E. and Jackson, P. (2014) Developmental coaching, in E. Cox, T. Bachkirova and D. Clutterbuck (eds.) *The Complete Handbook of Coaching*, 2nd edition, 215–227, London: Sage.

Creswell, J.W. (2010) *Designing and Conducting Mixed Methods Research*, 2nd edition, London: Sage.

Deci, E. and Ryan, R.M. (1985) *Intrinsic Motivation and Self-determination in Human Behavior*, Dordrecht: Springer Science & Business Media.

De Haan, E., Bertie, C., Day, A. and Sills, C. (2010) Clients' critical moments of coaching: Toward a 'client model' of executive coaching, *Academy of Management Learning and Education*, 9 (4): 607–621.

De Haan, E. and Duckworth, A. (2013) Signalling a new trend in executive coaching outcome research, *International Coaching Psychology Review*, 8 (1): 6–19.

De Haan, E., Duckworth, A., Birch, D. and Jones, C. (2013) Executive coaching outcome research: The contribution of common factors such as relationship, personality match, and self-efficacy, *Consulting Psychology Journal: Practice and Research*, 65 (1): 40–57.

De Haan, E. and Gannon, J. (2016) The Coaching Relationship, in T. Bachkirova, G. Spence and D. Drake (eds.) *The SAGE Handbook of Coaching*, 195–220, London: Sage.

De Haan, E., Grant, A.M., Burger, Y. and Eriksson, P.-O. (2016) A large-scale study of executive and workplace coaching: The relative contributions of relationship, personality match, and self-efficacy, *Consulting Psychology Journal: Practice and Research*, 68 (3): 189–207.

De Haan, E. and Nieß, C. (2015) Differences between critical moments for clients, coaches, and sponsors of coaching, *International Coaching Psychology Review*, 10 (1): 38–61.

De Haan, E. and Nilsson, V.O. (2017) Evaluating coaching behavior in managers, consultants, and coaches: A model, questionnaire, and initial findings, *Consulting Psychology Journal: Practice and Research*, 69 (4): 315–333.

Dewey, J. (1910) Science as subject-matter and as method, *Science*, 31 (787): 121–127.

Diggins, J.P. (1994) *The Promise of Pragmatism: Modernism and the crisis of knowledge and authority*, Chicago, IL: University of Chicago Press.

Ditto, P.H. and Lopez, D.F. (1992) Motivated skepticism: Use of differential decision criteria for preferred and nonpreferred conclusions, *Journal of Personality and Social Psychology*, 63 (4): 568–584.

Drake, D.B. (2011) What do coaches need to know? Using the mastery window to assess and develop expertise, *Coaching: An International Journal of Theory, Research and Practice*, 4 (2): 138–155.

Duncan, B.L., Miller, S.D., Wampold, B.E. and Hubble, M.A. (2010) *The Heart & Soul of Change: Delivering what works in therapy*, 2nd edition, Washington, DC: American Psychological Association.

Dweck, C.S. and Leggett, E.L. (1988) A social-cognitive approach to motivation and personality, *Psychological Review*, 95 (2): 256–273.

Eby, L.T., Allen, T.D., Hoffman, B.J., Baranik, L.E., Sauer, J.B., Baldwin, S. et al. (2013) An interdisciplinary meta-analysis of the potential antecedents, correlates, and consequences of protégé perceptions of mentoring, *Psychological Bulletin*, 139 (2): 441–476.

Ellinger, A.D., Ellinger, A.E. and Keller, S.B. (2003) Supervisory coaching behavior, employee satisfaction, and warehouse employee performance: A dyadic perspective in the distribution industry, *Human Resource Development Quarterly*, 14 (4): 435–458.

Ely, K., Boyce, L.A., Nelson, J.K., Zaccaro, S.J., Hernez-Broome, G. and Whyman, W. (2010) Evaluating leadership coaching: A review and integrated framework, *Leadership Quarterly*, 21 (4): 585–599.

Ericsson, K.A., Charness, N., Feltovich, P.J. and Hoffman, R.R. (eds.) (2006) *The Cambridge Handbook of Expertise and Expert Performance*, Cambridge: Cambridge University Press.

Ewenstein, B., Hancock, B. and Komm, A. (2016) Ahead of the curve: The future of performance management, *McKinsey Quarterly*, 16 May. Available at: https://www.mckinsey.com/business-functions/organization/our-insights/ahead-of-the-curve-the-future-of-performance-management.

Feldman, D.C. and Lankau, M.J. (2005) Executive coaching: A review and agenda for future research, *Journal of Management*, 31 (6): 829–848.

Fletcher, R.B. and Roberts, M.H. (2013) Longitudinal stability of the Leadership Scale for Sports, *Measurement in Physical Education and Exercise Science*, 17 (2): 89–104.

Fredrickson, B.L. (2001) The role of positive emotions in positive psychology: The broaden-and-build theory of positive emotions, *American Psychologist*, 56 (3): 218–226.

Gaertner, H. (2014) Effects of student feedback as a method of self-evaluating the quality of teaching, *Studies in Educational Evaluation*, 42: 91–99.

Gettman, H.J., Edinger, S.K. and Wouters, K. (2019) Assessing contracting and the coaching relationship: Necessary infrastructure?, *International Journal of Evidence Based Coaching and Mentoring*, 17 (1): 46–62.

Grant, A.M. (2014) The efficacy of executive coaching in times of organizational change, *Journal of Change Management*, 14 (2): 258–280.

Grant, A.M. (2016) What can Sydney tell us about coaching? Research with implications for practice from down under, *Consulting Psychology Journal: Practice and Research*, 68 (2): 105–117.

Grant, A.M. and Cavanagh, M.J. (2007) Evidence-based coaching: Flourishing or languishing?, *Australian Psychologist*, 42 (4): 239–254.

Grant, A.M., Franklin, J. and Langford, P. (2002) The Self-Reflection and Insight Scale: A new measure of private self-consciousness, *Social Behavior and Personality: An International Journal*, 30 (8): 821–835.

Greenberg, L.S. (1980) Training counsellors in Gestalt methods, *Canadian Journal of Counselling and Psychotherapy*, 14 (3). Available at: https://cjc-rcc.ucalgary.ca/article/view/60340.

Greif, S. (2016) Researching outcomes of coaching, in T. Bachkirova, G. Spence and D. Drake (eds.) *The SAGE Handbook of Coaching*, 571–590, London: Sage.

Grover, S. and Furnham, A. (2016) Coaching as a developmental intervention in organizations: A systematic review of its effectiveness and the mechanisms underlying it, *PLoS One*, 11 (7): e0159137. Available at: https://doi.org/10.1371/journal.pone.0159137.

Gyllensten, K. and Palmer, S. (2007) The coaching relationship: An interpretative phenomenological analysis, *International Coaching Psychology Review*, 2 (2): 168–177.

Halpern, H. (2009) Supervision and the Johari window: A framework for asking questions, *Education for Primary Care*, 20 (1): 10–14.

Hawkins, P. and Smith, N. (2013) *Coaching, Mentoring and Organizational Consultancy: Supervision, skills and development*, 2nd edition, Maidenhead: Open University Press.

Hay, J. (2007) *Reflective Practice and Supervision for Coaches*, Maidenhead: Open University Press.

Heron, J. (2001) *Helping the Client: A creative practical guide*, London: Sage.

Hofstede, G. (1980) *Culture's Consequences: International Differences in Work-Related Values*, Beverly Hills, CA: Sage.

Hóigaard, R., Jones, G. and Peters, D.M. (2008) Preferred coach leadership behaviour in elite soccer in relation to success and failure, *International Journal of Sports Science and Coaching*, 3 (2): 241–250.

Hooijberg, R. and Lane, N. (2009) Using multisource feedback coaching effectively in executive education, *Academy of Management Learning and Education*, 8 (4): 483–493.

Hullinger, A.M. and DiGirolamo, J.A. (2020) A professional development study: The lifelong journeys of coaches, *International Psychology Review*, 15 (1): 8–19.

Hullinger, A.M., DiGirolamo, J.A. and Tkach, J.T. (2019) Reflective practice for coaches and clients: An integrated model for learning, *Philosophy of Coaching: An International Journal*, 4 (2): 5–34.

Ianiro, P., Lehmann-Willenbrock, N. and Kauffeld, S. (2015) Coaches and clients in action: A sequential analysis of interpersonal coach and client behaviour, *Journal of Business and Psychology*, 30 (3): 435–456.

Ianiro, P.M., Schermuly, C.C. and Kauffeld, S. (2013) Why interpersonal dominance and affiliation matter: An interaction analysis of the coach–client relationship, *Coaching: An International Journal of Theory, Research and Practice*, 6 (1): 25–46.

International Coach Federation (ICF) (2019) *Core Competencies*. Available at: https://coachfederation.org/core-competencies [accessed 2 November 2019].

International Coach Federation (ICF) (2020a) *Coaching Supervision*. Available at: https://coachfederation.org/coaching-supervision.

International Coach Federation (ICF) (2020b) *Mentor Coaching*. Available at: https://coachfederation.org/mentor-coaching.

International Coach Federation and PricewaterhouseCoopers (ICF/PwC) (2016) *ICF Global Coaching Study*. Available at: https://coachfederation.org/app/uploads/2017/12/2016ICFGlobalCoachingStudy_ExecutiveSummary-2.pdf [accessed 2 March 2017].

Jackson, D.J.R., Lance, C.E. and Hoffman, B.J. (2012) *The Psychology of Assessment Centers*, New York: Routledge.

Jawahar, I. (2010) The mediating role of appraisal feedback reactions on the relationship between rater feedback-related behaviors and ratee performance, *Group and Organization Management*, 35 (4): 494–526.

Jones, C. (2015) *Choosing your coach: What matters and when. An interpretative phenomenological exploration of the voice of the coachee*, Unpublished PhD dissertation, Oxford: Oxford Brookes University.

Jones, R.J., Woods, S.A. and Guillaume, Y.R.F. (2016) The effectiveness of workplace coaching: A meta-analysis of learning and performance outcomes from coaching, *Journal of Occupational and Organizational Psychology*, 89 (2): 249–277.

Karboul, A. (2014) *Experiencing coaching for the first time: First coaching sessions from the executive clients' perspective*, Unpublished PhD dissertation, Oxford: Oxford Brookes University.

Kasser, T. and Ryan, R.M. (1993) A dark side of the American dream: Correlates of financial success as a central life aspiration, *Journal of Personality and Social Psychology*, 65 (2): 410–422.

Kauffeld, S. and Gessnitzer, S. (2015) The working alliance in coaching: Why behavior is the key to success, *Journal of Applied Behavioral Science*, 51 (2): 177–197.

Kegan, R. (1982) *The Evolving Self: Problem and process in human development*, Cambridge, MA: Harvard University Press.

Kegan, R. and Lahey, L.L. (2001) The real reason people won't change, *Harvard Business Review*, November. Available at: https://hbr.org/2001/11/the-real-reason-people-wont-change.

Kets De Vries, M.F.R. (2013) Coaching's good hour: Creating tipping points, *Coaching: An International Journal of Theory, Research and Practice*, 6 (2): 152–175.

Kilburg, R.R. (2016) The development of human expertise: Toward a model for the 21st-century practice of coaching, consulting, and general applied psychology, *Consulting Psychology Journal: Practice and Research*, 68 (2): 177–187.

King, E. and Nesbit, P. (2015) Collusion with denial: Leadership development and its evaluation, *Journal of Management Development*, 34 (2): 134–152.

Kirkpatrick, D.L. (1977) Evaluating training programs: Evidence vs. proof, *Training and Development Journal*, 31 (11): 9–12.

Kluger, A.N. and Denisi, A. (1996) The effects of feedback interventions on performance: A historical review, a meta-analysis, and a preliminary feedback intervention theory, *Psychological Bulletin*, 119 (2): 254–284.

Knowles, M.S., Holton, E.F. and Swanson, R.A. (2011) *The Adult Learner: The definitive classic in adult education and human resource development*, 7th edition, Oxford: Butterworth-Heinemann.

Kolb, D.A. (1984) *Experiential Learning: Experience as the source of learning and development*, Englewood Cliffs, NJ: Prentice-Hall.

Lai, Y.-L. and McDowall, A. (2014) A systematic review of coaching psychology: Focusing on the attributes of effective coaching psychologists, *International Coaching Psychology Review*, 9 (2): 118–134.

Laloux, F. (2014) *Reinventing Organizations: A guide to creating organizations inspired by the next stage in human consciousness*, Brussels: Nelson Parker.

Lane, D.A. (2016) Trends in the development of coaches, in T. Bachkirova, G. Spence and D. Drake (eds.) *The SAGE Handbook of Coaching*, 649–663, London: Sage.

Larose, S., Bernier, A. and Soucy, N. (2005) Attachment as a moderator of the effect of security in mentoring on subsequent perceptions of mentoring and relationship quality with college teachers, *Journal of Social and Personal Relationships*, 22 (3): 399–415.

Laske, O.E. (2006) *Measuring Hidden Dimensions: The art and science of fully engaging adults*, Medford, MA: Interdevelopmental Institute Press.

Lawrence, P. (2016) Coaching and adult development, in T. Bachkirova, G. Spence and D. Drake (eds.) *The SAGE Handbook of Coaching*, 121–138, London: Sage.

Lawrence, P. and Whyte, A. (2014) Return on investment in executive coaching: A practical model for measuring ROI in organizations, *Coaching: An International Journal of Theory, Research and Practice*, 7 (1): 4–17.

Levenson, A. (2009) Measuring and maximising the business impact of executive coaching, *Consulting Psychology Journal: Practice and Research*, 61 (2): 103–121.

Levinson, H. (1996) Executive coaching, *Consulting Psychology Journal: Practice and Research*, 48 (2): 115–123.

Levitt, H.M., Pomerville, A. and Surace, F.I. (2016) A qualitative meta-analysis examining clients' experiences of psychotherapy: A new agenda, *Psychological Bulletin*, 142 (8): 801–830.

Lewis-Duarte, M. and Bligh, M.C. (2012) Agents of 'influence': Exploring the usage, timing, and outcomes of executive coaching tactics, *Leadership and Organization Development Journal*, 33 (3): 255–281.

Lievens, F. and Christiansen, N. (2012) Core debates in assessment center research: Dimensions versus exercises, in D.J.R. Jackson, C.E. Lance and B.J. Hoffman (eds.) *The Psychology of Assessment Centers*, 68–94, New York: Routledge.

Linder-Pelz, S. and Lawley, J. (2015) Using clean language to explore the subjectivity of coachees' experience and outcomes, *International Coaching Psychology Review*, 10 (2): 161–174.

Linder-Pelz, S. and Lawley, J. (2016) Evidence of competency: Exploring coach, coachee and expert evaluations of coaching, *Coaching: An International Journal of Theory, Research and Practice*, 9 (2): 110–128.

Luft, J. and Ingham, H. (1961) The Johari window, *Human Relations Training News*, 5 (1): 6–7.

Mabe, P.A. and West, S.G. (1982) Validity of self-evaluation of ability: A review and meta-analysis, *Journal of Applied Psychology*, 67 (3): 280–296.

MacKie, D. (2007) Evaluating the effectiveness of executive coaching: Where are we now and where do we need to be?, *Australian Psychologist*, 42 (4): 310–318.

Maltbia, T.E., Marsick, V.J. and Ghosh, R. (2014) Executive and organizational coaching, *Advances in Developing Human Resources*, 16 (2): 161–183.

Mandouit, L. (2018) Using student feedback to improve teaching, *Educational Action Research*, 26 (5): 755–769.

Marjanovic, Z., Struthers, C.W. and Greenglass, E.R. (2012) Who helps natural-disaster victims? Assessment of trait and situational predictors, *Analyses of Social Issues and Public Policy*, 12 (1): 245–267.

Maxwell, A. (2016) The use of feedback for development in coaching: Finding the coach's stance, in T. Bachkirova, G. Spence and D. Drake (eds.) *The SAGE Handbook of Coaching*, 312–332, London: Sage.

McAllister, D.J. (1995) Affect- and cognition-based trust as foundations for interpersonal cooperation in organizations, *Academy of Management Journal*, 38 (1): 24–59.

McCay-Peet, L. and Toms, E.G. (2011) The serendipity quotient, *Proceedings of the American Society for Information Science and Technology*, 48 (1): 1–4.

McDowall, A. and Smewing, C. (2009) What assessments do coaches use in their practice and why?, *Coaching Psychologist*, 5 (2): 98–103.

Mezirow, J. (1990) *Fostering Critical Reflection in Adulthood: A guide to transformational and emancipatory learning*, San Francisco, CA: Jossey-Bass.

Miller, S.D., Hubble, M.A., Chow, D. and Seidel, J. (2015) Beyond measures and monitoring: Realising the potential of feedback-informed treatment, *Psychotherapy*, 52 (4): 449–457.

Minski, C.-A. (2015) *Executive Coaching and Self-efficacy: A study of goal-setting and leadership capacity*, Ann Arbor, MI: ProQuest LLC.

Mischel, W. and Shoda, Y. (1995) A cognitive-affective system theory of personality: Reconceptualising situations, dispositions, dynamics, and invariance in personality structure, *Psychological Review*, 102 (2): 246–268.

Moons, J. (2015) *Shift in the room – Myth or magic? How do coaches create a transformational shift in the room?*, Unpublished MA dissertation, Oxford: Oxford Brookes University.

Morozov, E. (2016) Evgeny Morozov. L'intellectuel du Net dégaine, *Philosophie Magazine*, 97 (March). Available at: https://www.philomag.com/articles/evgeny-morozov-lintellectuel-du-net-degaine.

Mulvie, A. (2015) *The Value of Executive Coaching*, London: Routledge.

Myers, A.C. (2014) *A multiple perspective analysis of a coaching session*, Unpublished PhD thesis, Oxford: Oxford Brookes University.

Myers, A. and Bachkirova, T. (2020) The Rashomon effect in the perception of coaching sessions and what this means for the evaluation of the quality: a grounded theory study, *Coaching: An International Journal of Theory, Research and Practice*, 13 (1): 92–105.

Nicolaides, A. and McCallum, D. (2013) Inquiry in action for leadership in turbulent times: Exploring the connections between transformational learning and adaptive leadership, *Journal of Transformational Education*, 11 (4): 246–260.

Nieminen, L.R.G., Smerek, R., Kotrba, L. and Denison, D. (2013) What does an executive coaching intervention add beyond facilitated multisource feedback? Effects on leader self-ratings and perceived effectiveness, *Human Resource Development Quarterly*, 24 (2): 145–176.

Norcross, J.C. (2010) The therapeutic relationship, in B.L. Duncan, S.D. Miller, B.E. Wampold and M.A. Hubble (eds.) *The Heart and Soul of Change: Delivering what works in therapy*, 2nd edition, 118–131, Washington, DC: American Psychological Association.

O'Broin, A. and Palmer, S. (2010) Exploring key aspects in the formation of coaching relationships: Initial indicators from the perspective of the coachee and the coach, *Coaching: An International Journal of Theory, Research and Practice*, 3 (2): 124–143.

O'Neill, M.B. (2007) *Executive Coaching with Backbone and Heart: A systems approach to engaging leaders with their challenges*, San Francisco, CA: Jossey-Bass.

Onwuegbuzie, A.J., Witcher, A.E., Collins, K.M.T., Filer, J.D., Wiedmaier, C.D. and Moore, C.W. (2007) Students' perceptions of characteristics of effective college teachers: A validity study of a teaching evaluation form using a mixed-methods analysis, *American Educational Research Journal*, 44 (1): 113–160.

Passmore, J., Brown, H., Wall, T., Stokes, P. and the European Coaching and Mentoring Research Consortium (2018) *The State of Play in Coaching in the United Kingdom*, Henley-on-Thames: Henley Business School.

Passmore, J. and Fillery-Travis, A. (2011) A critical review of executive coaching research: A decade of progress and what's to come, *Coaching: An International Journal of Theory, Research and Practice*, 4 (2): 70–88.

Peterson, D.B. (1993) *Measuring change: A psychometric approach to evaluating individual coaching outcomes*, Presented at the Annual Conference of the Society for Industrial and Organizational Psychology, 30 April, San Francisco, CA.

Reese, R.J., Usher, E.L., Bowman, D.C., Norsworthy, L.A., Halstead, J.L., Rowlands, S.R. et al. (2009) Using client feedback in psychotherapy training: An analysis of its influence on supervision and counselor self-efficacy, *Training and Education in Professional Psychology*, 3 (3): 157–168.

Rekalde, I., Landeta, J. and Albizu, E. (2015) Determining factors in the effectiveness of executive coaching as a management development tool, *Management Decision*, 53 (8): 1677–1697.

Renato Railo, R. (2015) Resenha: Manifesto del Nuovo Realismo, de Maurizio Ferraris, *Aufklärung*, 2 (1): 209–218.

Richardson, J.T.E. (2005) Instruments for obtaining student feedback: A review of the literature, *Assessment and Evaluation in Higher Education*, 30 (4): 387–415.

Riddle, D., Hoole, E.R. and Gullette, E.C. (2015) *The Center for Creative Leadership Handbook of Coaching in Organizations*, New York: Wiley.

Rogers, C.R. (1957) The necessary and sufficient conditions of therapeutic personality change, *Journal of Consulting Psychology*, 21 (2): 95–103.

Rojon, C. and McDowall, A. (2010) Cultural Orientations Framework (COF) assessment questionnaire in cross-cultural coaching: A cross-validation with Wave Focus Styles, *International Journal of Evidence Based Coaching and Mentoring*, 8 (2): 1–26.

Rousseau, D.M. (1998) The 'problem' of the psychological contract considered, *Journal of Organizational Behavior*, 19 (suppl. 1): 665–671.

Sammut, K. (2014) Transformational learning theory and coaching: Application in practice, *International Journal of Evidence Based Coaching and Mentoring*, S8: 39–53.

Schippmann, J.S., Ash, R.A., Battista, M., Carr, L., Eyde, L.D., Hesketh, B. et al. (2000) The practice of competency modelling, *Personnel Psychology*, 53 (3): 703–740.

Schön, D.A. (1984) *The Reflective Practitioner: How professionals think in action*, New York: Basic Books.

Seiler, H. (2019) The client as a provider of developmental feedback for the executive coach, *International Journal of Evidence Based Coaching and Mentoring*, S13: 114–125.

Senge, P., Hamilton, H. and Kania, J. (2015) The dawn of system leadership, *Stanford Social Innovation Review*, 13 (1): 27–33.

Sheldon, K.M. and Elliot, A.J. (1998) Not all personal goals are personal: Comparing autonomous and controlled reasons for goals as predictors of effort and attainment, *Personality and Social Psychology Bulletin*, 24 (5): 546–557.

Sherpa Coaching (2018) *The 2018 Executive Coaching Survey: Full report.* Cincinnati, OH: Sherpa Coaching, LLC.

Sieler, A. (2003) *Coaching to the Human Soul: Ontological coaching and deep change*, Blackburn, VIC: Newfield Institute.

Skinner, B.F. (1990) Can psychology be a science of mind?, *American Psychologist*, 45 (11): 1206–1210.

Smith, I.M. and Brummel, B.J. (2013) Investigating the role of the active ingredients in executive coaching, *Coaching: An International Journal of Theory, Research and Practice*, 6 (1): 57–71.

Sonesh, S.C., Coultas, C.W., Lacerenza, C.N., Marlow, S.L., Benishek, L.E. and Salas, E. (2015a) The power of coaching: A meta-analytic investigation, *Coaching: An International Journal of Theory, Research and Practice*, 8 (2): 73–95.

Sonesh, S.C., Coultas, C.W., Marlow, S.L., Lacerenza, C.N., Reyes, D. and Salas, E. (2015b) Coaching in the wild: Identifying factors that lead to success, *Consulting Psychology Journal: Practice and Research*, 67 (3): 189–217.

Stalmeijer, R.E., Dolmans, D.H.J.M., Wolfhagen, I.H.A.P., Muijtjens, A.M.M. and Scherpbier, A.J.J.A. (2008) The development of an instrument for evaluating clinical teachers: Involving stakeholders to determine content validity, *Medical Teacher*, 30 (8): e272–e277.

Sternberg, R.J. and Lubart, T.I. (1995) *Defying the Crowd: Cultivating creativity in a culture of conformity*, New York: Free Press.

Stokes, P. (2015) *The Skilled Coachee: An alternative discourse on coach*, Sheffield: Sheffield Business School.

Theeboom, T., Beersma, B. and Van Vianen, A.E.M. (2014) Does coaching work? A meta-analysis on the effects of coaching on individual level outcomes in an organizational context, *Journal of Positive Psychology*, 9 (1): 1–18.

Theeboom, T., Van Vianen, A.E.M. and Beersma, B. (2017) A temporal map of coaching, *Frontiers in Psychology*, 8: 1352. Available at: https://doi.org/10.3389/fpsyg.2017.01352.

Thurlings, M., Vermeulen, M., Bastiaens, T. and Stijnen, S. (2013) Understanding feedback: A learning theory perspective, *Educational Research Review*, 9: 1–15.

Tkach, J.T. and DiGirolamo, J.A. (2017) The state and future of coaching supervision, *International Coaching Psychology Review*, 12 (1): 49–63.

Tonomura, I., Raubien, A. and Sato, Y.I. (2018) *How executives succeed through executive coaching.* Available at: https://cri.coacha.com/en/research/reports/cses2015.pdf [accessed 24 June 2018].

Turner, E. and Hawkins, P. (2016) Multi-stakeholder contracting in executive/business coaching: An analysis of practice and recommendations for gaining maximum value, *International Journal of Evidence Based Coaching and Mentoring*, 14 (2): 48–65.

Vandaveer, V.V., Lowman, R.L., Pearlman, K. and Brannick, J.P. (2016) A practice analysis of coaching psychology: Toward a foundational competency model, *Consulting Psychology Journal: Practice and Research*, 68 (2): 118–142.

Van Nieuwerburgh, C. (2016) Interculturally-sensitive coaching, in T. Bachkirova, G. Spence and D. Drake (eds.) *The SAGE Handbook of Coaching*, 439–452, London: Sage.

Welman, P. and Bachkirova, T. (2010) The issue of power in the coaching relationship, in S. Palmer and A. McDowall (eds.) *The Coaching Relationship: Putting people first. Essential coaching skills and knowledge*, 139–158, Hove: Routledge.

Western, S. (2012) *Coaching and Mentoring: A critical text*, Thousand Oaks, CA: Sage.

Whitworth, L., Kimsey-House, K., Kimsey-House, H. and Sandahl, P. (2007) *Co-active Coaching*, Mountain View, CA: Davies-Black.

Wiener, N. (1961) *Cybernetics or Control and Communication in the Animal and the Machine*, 2nd edition, Cambridge, MA: MIT Press.

Wilkins, P. (2000) Unconditional positive regard reconsidered, *British Journal of Guidance and Counselling*, 28 (1): 23–36.

Will, T., Gessnitzer, S. and Kauffeld, S. (2016) You think you are an empathic coach? Maybe you should think again. The difference between perceptions of empathy vs. empathic behaviour after a person-centred coaching training, *Coaching: An International Journal of Theory, Research and Practice*, 9 (1): 53–68.

Yu, J. and Murphy, K. (1993) Modesty bias in self-ratings of performance: A test of the cultural relativity hypothesis, *Personnel Psychology*, 46 (2): 357–363.

Zohar, D. and Marshall, I. (2001) *Spiritual Intelligence: The ultimate intelligence*, London: Bloomsbury.

Index